Wonderful ways to prepare

FOOD
FOR FREEZING

by JO ANN SHIRLEY

Wonderful ways to prepare

FOOD
FOR FREEZING

PLAYMORE INC. NEW YORK USA
UNDER ARRANGEMENT WITH
WALDMAN PUBLISHING CORP.

AYERS & JAMES
SYDNEY AUSTRALIA

STAFFORD PEMBERTON PUBLISHING
KNUTSFORD UNITED KINGDOM

FIRST PUBLISHED 1979

PUBLISHED IN THE USA
BY PLAYMORE INC.
UNDER ARRANGEMENT WITH
WALDMAN PUBLISHING CORP.

PUBLISHED IN AUSTRALIA
BY AYERS & JAMES
CROWS NEST.   AUSTRALIA

PUBLISHED IN THE UNITED KINGDOM
BY STAFFORD PEMBERTON PUBLISHING
KNUTSFORD CHESHIRE

ISBN 0 86908 155 1

OVEN TEMPERATURE GUIDE

Description	Gas		Electric		Mark
	C	F	C	F	
Cool	100	200	110	225	¼
Very Slow	120	250	120	250	½
Slow	150	300	150	300	1-2
Moderately slow	160	325	170	340	3
Moderate	180	350	200	400	4
Moderately hot	190	375	220	425	5-6
Hot	200	400	230	450	6-7
Very hot	230	450	250	475	8-9

LIQUID MEASURES

IMPERIAL	METRIC
1 teaspoon	5 ml
1 tablespoon	20 ml
2 fluid ounces (½ cup)	62.5 ml
4 fluid ounces (½ cup)	125 ml
8 fluid ounces (1 cup)	250 ml
1 pint (16 ounces — 2 cups)*	500 ml

* (The imperial pint is equal to 20 fluid ounces.)

SOLID MEASURES

AVOIRDUPOIS	METRIC
1 ounce	30 g
4 ounces (¼ lb)	125 g
8 ounces (½ lb)	250 g
12 ounces (¾ lb)	375 g
16 ounces (1 lb)	500 g
24 ounces (1½ lb)	750 g
32 ounces (2 lb)	1000 g (1 kg)

CUP AND SPOON REPLACEMENTS FOR OUNCES

INGREDIENT	½ oz	1 oz	2 oz	3 oz	4 oz	5 oz	6 oz	7 oz	8 oz
Almonds, ground	2 T	¼ C	½ C	¾ C	1¼ C	1⅓ C	1⅔ C	2 C	2¼ C
slivered	6 t	¼ C	½ C	¾ C	1 C	1⅓ C	1⅔ C	2 C	2¼ C
whole	2 T	¼ C	⅓ C	½ C	¾ C	1 C	1¼ C	1⅓ C	1½ C
Apples, dried whole	3 T	½ C	1 C	1⅓ C	2 C	2⅓ C	2¾ C	3⅓ C	3¾ C
Apricots, chopped	2 T	¼ C	½ C	¾ C	1 C	1¼ C	1½ C	1¾ C	2 C
whole	2 T	3 T	½ C	⅔ C	1 C	1¼ C	1⅓ C	1½ C	1¾ C
Arrowroot	1 T	2 T	⅓ C	½ C	⅔ C	¾ C	1 C	1¼ C	1⅓ C
Baking Powder	1 T	2 T	⅓ C	½ C	⅔ C	¾ C	1 C	1 C	1¼ C
Baking Soda	1 T	2 T	⅓ C	½ C	⅔ C	¾ C	1 C	1 C	1¼ C
Barley	1 T	2 T	¼ C	½ C	⅔ C	¾ C	1 C	1 C	1¼ C
Breadcrumbs, dry	2 T	¼ C	½ C	¾ C	1 C	1¼ C	1½ C	1¾ C	2 C
soft	¼ C	½ C	1 C	1½ C	2 C	2½ C	3 C	3⅔ C	4¼ C
Biscuit Crumbs	2 T	¼ C	½ C	¾ C	1¼ C	1⅓ C	1⅔ C	2 C	2¼ C
Butter	3 t	6 t	¼ C	⅓ C	½ C	⅔ C	¾ C	1 C	1 C
Cheese, grated, lightly packed,									
natural cheddar	6 t	¼ C	½ C	¾ C	1 C	1¼ C	1½ C	1¾ C	2 C
Processed cheddar	5 t	2 T	⅓ C	⅔ C	¾ C	1 C	1¼ C	1½ C	1⅔ C
Parmesan, Romano	6 t	¼ C	½ C	¾ C	1 C	1⅓ C	1⅔ C	2 C	2¼ C
Cherries, candied, chopped	1 T	2 T	⅓ C	½ C	¾ C	1 C	1 C	1⅓ C	1½ C
whole	1 T	2 T	⅓ C	½ C	⅔ C	¾ C	1 C	1¼ C	1⅓ C
Cocoa	2 T	¼ C	½ C	¾ C	1¼ C	1⅓ C	1⅔ C	2 C	2¼ C
Coconut, desiccated	2 T	⅓ C	⅔ C	1 C	1⅓ C	1⅔ C	2 C	2⅓ C	2⅔ C
shredded	⅓ C	⅔ C	1¼ C	1¾ C	2½ C	3 C	3⅔ C	4⅓ C	5 C
Cornstarch	6 t	3 T	½ C	⅔ C	1 C	1¼ C	1½ C	1⅔ C	2 C
Corn Syrup	2 t	1 T	2 T	¼ C	⅓ C	½ C	½ C	⅔ C	⅔ C
Coffee, ground	2 T	⅓ C	⅔ C	1 C	1⅓ C	1⅔ C	2 C	2⅓ C	2⅔ C
instant	3 T	½ C	1 C	1⅓ C	1¾ C	2¼ C	2⅔ C	3 C	3½ C
Cornflakes	½ C	1 C	2 C	3 C	4¼ C	5¼ C	6¼ C	7⅓C	8⅓ C
Cream of Tartar	1 T	2 T	⅓ C	½ C	⅔ C	¾ C	1 C	1 C	1¼ C
Currants	1 T	2 T	⅓ C	⅔ C	¾ C	1 C	1¼ C	1½ C	1⅔ C
Custard Powder	6 t	3 T	½ C	⅔ C	1 C	1¼ C	1½ C	1⅔ C	2 C
Dates, chopped	1 T	2 T	⅓ C	⅔ C	¾ C	1 C	1¼ C	1½ C	1⅔ C
whole, pitted	1 T	2 T	⅓ C	½ C	¾ C	1 C	1¼ C	1⅓ C	1½ C
Figs, chopped	1 T	2 T	⅓ C	½ C	¾ C	1 C	1 C	1⅓ C	1½ C
Flour, all-purpose or cake	6 t	¼ C	½ C	¾ C	1 C	1¼ C	1½ C	1¾ C	2 C
wholemeal	6 t	3 T	½ C	⅔ C	1 C	1¼ C	1⅓ C	1⅔ C	1¾ C
Fruit, mixed	1 T	2 T	⅓ C	½ C	¾ C	1 C	1¼ C	1⅓ C	1½ C
Gelatin	5 t	2 T	⅓ C	½ C	¾ C	1 C	1 C	1¼ C	1½ C
Ginger, crystallised pieces	1 T	2 T	⅓ C	½ C	¾ C	1 C	1¼ C	1⅓ C	1½ C
ground	6 t	⅓ C	½ C	¾ C	1¼ C	1½ C	1¾ C	2 C	2¼ C
preserved, heavy syrup	1 T	2 T	⅓ C	½ C	⅔ C	¾ C	1 C	1 C	1¼ C
Glucose, liquid	2 t	1 T	2 T	¼ C	⅓ C	½ C	½ C	⅔ C	⅔ C
Haricot Beans	1 T	2 T	⅓ C	½ C	⅔ C	¾ C	1 C	1 C	1¼ C

In this table, t represents teaspoonful, T represents tablespoonful and C represents cupful.

CUP AND SPOON REPLACEMENTS FOR OUNCES (Cont.)

INGREDIENT	½ oz	1 oz	2 oz	3 oz	4 oz	5 oz	6 oz	7 oz	8 oz
Honey	2 t	1 T	2 T	¼ C	⅓ C	½ C	½ C	⅔ C	⅔ C
Jam	2 t	1 T	2 T	¼ C	⅓ C	½ C	½ C	⅔ C	¾ C
Lentils	1 T	2 T	⅓ C	½ C	⅔ C	¾ C	1 C	1 C	1¼ C
Macaroni (see pasta)									
Milk Powder, full cream	2 T	¼ C	½ C	¾ C	1¼ C	1⅓ C	1⅔ C	2 C	2¼ C
non fat	2 T	⅓ C	¾ C	1¼ C	1½ C	2 C	2⅓ C	2¾ C	3¼ C
Nutmeg	6 t	3 T	½ C	⅔ C	¾ C	1 C	1¼ C	1½ C	1⅔ C
Nuts, chopped	6 t	¼ C	½ C	¾ C	1 C	1¼ C	1½ C	1¾ C	2 C
Oatmeal	1 T	2 T	½ C	⅔ C	¾ C	1 C	1¼ C	1½ C	1⅔ C
Olives, whole	1 T	2 T	⅓ C	⅔ C	¾ C	1 C	1¼ C	1½ C	1⅔ C
sliced	1 T	2 T	⅓ C	⅔ C	¾ C	1 C	1¼ C	1½ C	1⅔ C
Pasta, short (e.g. macaroni)	1 T	2 T	⅓ C	⅔ C	¾ C	1 C	1¼ C	1½ C	1⅔ C
Peaches, dried & whole	1 T	2 T	⅓ C	⅔ C	¾ C	1 C	1¼ C	1½ C	1⅔ C
chopped	6 t	¼ C	½ C	¾ C	1 C	1¼ C	1½ C	1¾ C	2 C
Peanuts, shelled, raw, whole	1 T	2 T	⅓ C	½ C	¾ C	1 C	1¼ C	1⅓ C	1½ C
roasted	1 T	2 T	⅓ C	⅔ C	¾ C	1 C	1¼ C	1½ C	1⅔ C
Peanut Butter	3 t	6 t	3 T	⅓ C	½ C	½ C	⅔ C	¾ C	1 C
Peas, split	1 T	2 T	⅓ C	½ C	⅔ C	¾ C	1 C	1 C	1¼ C
Peel, mixed	1 T	2 T	⅓ C	½ C	¾ C	1 C	1 C	1¼ C	1½ C
Potato, powder	1 T	2 T	¼ C	⅓ C	½ C	⅔ C	¾ C	1 C	1¼ C
flakes	¼ C	½ C	1 C	1⅓ C	2 C	2⅓ C	2¾ C	3⅓ C	3¾ C
Prunes, chopped	1 T	2 T	⅓ C	½ C	⅔ C	¾ C	1 C	1¼ C	1⅓ C
whole pitted	1 T	2 T	⅓ C	½ C	⅔ C	¾ C	1 C	1 C	1¼ C
Raisins	2 T	¼ C	⅓ C	½ C	¾ C	1 C	1 C	1⅓ C	1½ C
Rice, short grain, raw	1 T	2 T	¼ C	½ C	⅔ C	¾ C	1 C	1 C	1¼ C
long grain, raw	1 T	2 T	⅓ C	½ C	¾ C	1 C	1¼ C	1⅓ C	1½ C
Rice Bubbles	⅔ C	1¼ C	2½ C	3⅔ C	5 C	6¼ C	7½ C	8¾ C	10 C
Rolled Oats	2 T	⅓ C	⅔ C	1 C	1⅓ C	1¾ C	2 C	2½ C	2¾ C
Sago	2 T	¼ C	⅓ C	½ C	¾ C	1 C	1 C	1¼ C	1½ C
Salt, common	3 t	6 t	¼ C	⅓ C	½ C	⅔ C	¾ C	1 C	1 C
Semolina	1 T	2 T	⅓ C	½ C	¾ C	1 C	1 C	1⅓ C	1½ C
Spices	6 t	3 T	¼ C	⅓ C	½ C	½ C	⅔ C	¾ C	1 C
Sugar, plain	3 t	6 t	¼ C	⅓ C	½ C	⅔ C	¾ C	1 C	1 C
confectioners'	1 T	2 T	⅓ C	½ C	¾ C	1 C	1 C	1¼ C	1½ C
moist brown	1 T	2 T	⅓ C	½ C	¾ C	1 C	1 C	1⅓ C	1½ C
Tapioca	1 T	2 T	⅓ C	½ C	⅔ C	¾ C	1 C	1¼ C	1⅓ C
Treacle	2 t	1 T	2 T	¼ C	⅓ C	½ C	½ C	⅔ C	⅔ C
Walnuts, chopped	2 T	¼ C	½ C	¾ C	1 C	1¼ C	1½ C	1¾ C	2 C
halved	2 T	⅓ C	⅔ C	1 C	1¼ C	1½ C	1¾ C	2¼ C	2½ C
Yeast, dried	6 t	3 T	½ C	⅔ C	1 C	1¼ C	1⅓ C	1⅔ C	1¾ C
compressed	3 t	6 t	3 T	⅓ C	½ C	½ C	⅔ C	¾ C	1 C

In this table, t represents teaspoonful, T represents tablespoonful and C represents cupful.

Contents

General Hints for Freezing

Because freezing of foods does not kill the bacteria in the food, it is important that the foods used are very fresh. The utensils used in the preparation of the food must be as clean and sterile as possible.

It is a safe rule not to refreeze food in its same state. If you freeze raw meat, it is possible to thaw it, cook it (perhaps in a casserole or roast) and then freeze the cooked meat. The same applies to vegetables.

Packaging

All containers used must be moisture-proof and air-tight.

Plastic bags: must be moisture-proof and strong enough not to puncture or break with the weight of the food.

Cling plastic film: must entirely encase the food. It is good for putting in between layers of meat, fruit and vegetables.

Aluminum foil: should be the heavy-duty foil.

Foil containers: convenient because dishes can be put directly into the oven. Should not be used for acidic food such as rhubarb, lemon, etc.

Plastic containers: good for delicate food such as meringues and decorated cakes and easily damaged food such as strawberries. Good for sauces, casseroles and stews. Must seal well.

Waxed cartons: good for soups and liquids.

Sealing and Covering

Use tight-fitting lids for plastic containers; aluminum foil for dishes with lids; plastic film for foil containers. All covering should be sealed with special freezing tape to ensure that the package is air-tight.

It is important to draw out as much air as possible from the packages. Rigid containers should be filled with food so there is as little air as possible in the container. There should, however, be some space left in the top of containers holding stews and casseroles, gravies, liquids and fruits in syrup to allow for the expansion of the liquid during freezing.

If fruits float on the top of the syrup, put a piece of crumpled waxed paper on the top to hold the fruit under the syrup. It is easy to remove when the fruit is thawed.

An easy way to extract the air from a plastic bag is to close the neck of the bag around a straw and suck out the air. When the air is sucked out, pinch the straw just below the opening and close tightly. Seal with a wire twist-tie.

Another way to remove all the air is to submerge the plastic bag of food in a bowl of water. The weight of the water will force out all the air. Seal the bag tightly with a wire twist-tie, then lift out of the water.

Labelling

It is important to clearly label everything that you put into the freezer with the contents, the number of portions and the date of freezing. This will avoid a lot of confusion.

It is a good idea to keep a list of the foods in the freezer, the date you put it in, the number of each item (e.g. 6 × 1 lb packets of raw ground beef), the number taken out and the date by which it should be used.

While it is best to freeze fruit at its peak (when it is just ready for eating), over-ripe fruit can be pureed and used for sauces, desserts and baby food.

Potatoes and pasta are better added at the reheating stage of casseroles and stews where possible.

Garlic is better added at the reheating stage of any dish as it can create an "off" flavour.

Casseroles are more conveniently frozen in aluminum foil containers or in freezer-to-oven cookware as they can then be put directly into the oven and heated without thawing.

Since liquid expands during freezing, it is necessary to leave room at the top of any container to allow for this expansion.

First Courses

Avocado Soup

2 avocados
4 cups (1 liter) chicken stock
salt and pepper
pinch of nutmeg
²⁄₃ cup (165 ml) cream
chopped chives for garnish

1. Remove the skin and the stones from the avocados and dice.
2. Purée in an electric blender with the chicken stock or sieve through a strainer.
3. Put in a saucepan and simmer gently.
4. Season to taste with salt and pepper. Add nutmeg and mix well.
5. Remove from heat and stir in the cream. Cool.

To freeze: Pour into a plastic container and leave about ½ inch (1 cm) of space at the top to allow for expansion of the liquid during freezing. Seal well, label and freeze.

To serve: Allow to thaw at room temperature for about one hour. Soup should be cold when served. Garnish with chopped chives.

Serves 4.

Pea Soup with Ham

1 cup (200 g) split peas	1 cup chopped celery
3 tablespoons (45 g) butter	8 cups (2 liters) water
2 medium onions, chopped	1 bay leaf
1 cup diced ham	3 teaspoons salt
1 medium carrot, diced	

1. Soak the peas in enough water to cover overnight. Drain.
2. Melt the butter in large saucepan and saute the onion until golden brown.
3. Add the ham, carrot and celery and cook for another five minutes.
4. Add peas, water, bay leaf and celery and bring to a boil. Reduce heat, cover and simmer for about three hours. Remove the bay leaf and cool.

To freeze: Pour into a plastic container leaving about ½ inch (1 cm) of room at the top to allow for the expansion of the liquid during freezing. Seal well, label and freeze.

To serve: Thaw at room temperature for about 2 hours. Heat and serve.

Serves 6.

Cream of Chicken Soup

3 tablespoons (45 g) butter	1 cup chopped celery
5 tablespoons plain flour	2½ tablespoons chopped
5 cups (1¼ liters) chicken stock	parsley
2½ cups (625 ml) milk	salt and pepper

1. Melt the butter in a large saucepan.
2. Add the flour and stir well. Cook for about one minute over a low heat.
3. Slowly add half the chicken stock, stirring constantly. Bring to a boil.
4. Pour in the remaining stock and milk. Add the celery and parsley and season to taste with salt and pepper.
5. Bring to a boil. Reduce heat and simmer for ten minutes. Cool.

To freeze: Pour into a plastic container leaving about ½ inch (1 cm) of space at the top to allow for expansion of the liquid during the freezing process. Seal well, label and freeze.

To serve: Thaw at room temperature for about two hours. Heat and serve.

Serves 6.

Onion Soup

2 lb (1 kg) onions
4 tablespoons (60 g) butter
2½ tablespoons plain flour
8 cups (2 litres) beef stock

salt and pepper
fried rounds of bread
½ lb (250 g) cheese, grated

1. Saute the onions in the butter in a large saucepan until golden brown.
2. Add the flour and mix well.
3. Slowly add the beef stock, stirring constantly. Bring to a boil.
4. Season to taste with salt and pepper. Reduce heat, cover and simmer for 20 minutes. Cool.

To freeze: Skim any fat from the top of the soup. Put into a plastic container and allow 1 inch (2½ cm) of space at the top to allow for expansion of the liquid during the freezing. Seal, label and freeze.

To serve: Put the frozen soup in a saucepan and thaw over a very low heat. Bring to a boil. Put one round of fried bread on the bottom of each soup bowl, pour the soup over it and top with grated cheese. You may brown the cheese under a hot broiler or put in a very hot oven for five minutes.

Serves 8.

Vichyssoise

½ cup (125 g) butter
5 leeks, sliced
3 white onions, sliced
8 cups (2 liters) chicken
   stock
1½ lb (750 g) potatoes,
   peeled and diced

1½ cups diced celery
2 teaspoons salt
½ teaspoon pepper
2½ cups (625 ml) cream
chopped chives

1. Melt the butter in a large saucepan and saute the leeks and the onions for three minutes.
2. Add the chicken stock, potatoes, celery, salt and pepper and bring to a boil. Reduce heat, cover and simmer for ½ hour.
3. Sieve or purée in an electric blender. Cool. Skim off any fat.

To freeze: Put the soup in a plastic container leaving about 1 inch (2½ cm) of room at the top to allow for expansion of the liquid during freezing. Seal, label and freeze.

To serve: Allow soup to thaw in the refrigerator overnight. Keep chilled. Stir in the cream and garnish with chopped chives before serving.

Serves 8-10.

Tomato and Carrot Soup

1 tablespoon oil
2 medium onions, chopped
½ lb (250 g) carrots, sliced
½ cup chopped celery
½ cup peas
½ lb (250 g) tomatoes,
   peeled

1 bay leaf
1 teaspoon salt
¼ teaspoon pepper
4 cups (1 liter) water

1. Heat the oil and saute the onions until transparent.
2. Add the carrots and celery and cook until the onions are golden brown.
3. Add the remaining ingredients and bring to a boil. Reduce heat, cover and simmer for 45 minutes.
4. Remove the bay leaf and cool.

To freeze: Pour the soup into a plastic container leaving 1 inch (2½ cm) of space at the top to allow for expansion of the liquid during freezing. Seal, label and freeze.

To serve: Thaw at room temperature, then gently heat in a saucepan.

Serves 4.

Kidney Soup

3 tablespoons (45 g) butter
½ lb (250 g) lamb kidneys
1 medium onion, sliced
1 medium carrot, sliced
4 tablespoons chopped
   parsley

¼ teaspoon thyme
1 teaspoon salt
¼ teaspoon black pepper
4 cups (1 liter) beef stock
4 teaspoons cornstarch

1. Heat the butter in a large saucepan. Slice the kidneys and saute with the onion in the butter until the onion is golden brown.
2. Add the remaining ingredients except the cornstarch. Mix well and bring to a boil. Reduce heat, cover and simmer for about an hour.
3. Put through a sieve or purée in an electric blender.
4. Mix the cornstarch with a little water then add to the soup. Cool.

To freeze: Pour the soup into a plastic container leaving 1 inch (2½ cm) of room at the top to allow for the expansion of the liquid during the freezing. Seal, label and freeze.

To serve: Thaw the soup in the container at room temperature, then heat gently in a saucepan.

Serves 4.

Cucumber Soup

3 medium cucumbers
3 tablespoons (45 g) butter
salt and pepper
4 cups (1 liter) chicken
   stock

1 cup (250 g) sour cream
2½ tablespoons chopped
   parsley

1. Peel and chop the cucumbers.
2. Melt the butter and saute the cucumbers until soft.
3. Add the salt and pepper to taste and the chicken stock. Bring to a boil.
4. Sieve the soup or purée in an electric blender. Cool.

To freeze: Pour the soup into a plastic container leaving about 1 inch (2½ cm) of room at the top to allow for expansion during freezing. Seal, label and freeze.

To serve: Thaw in refrigerator overnight or for 12 hours. When thawed, stir in the sour cream and chopped parsley.

Serves 4-6.

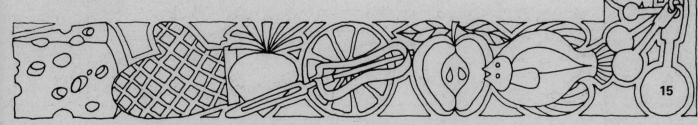

Oyster Soup

3 dozen small oysters
8 cups (2 liters) fish stock
strip of lemon rind
4 tablespoons (60 g) butter
½ cup plain flour

2 cups (500 ml) milk
1½ teaspoons lemon juice
1 teaspoon anchovy paste
4 teaspoons water
salt and pepper

1. Mix together the oysters, fish stock and lemon rind in a saucepan and simmer for 30 minutes. Strain and reserve the stock.
2. Melt the butter in a saucepan and stir in the flour. Cook gently for about one minute.
3. Slowly add the reserved stock to the butter and flour, stirring constantly. **Bring to a boil.**
4. Add the milk and the lemon juice mixed with the anchovy paste and water. Season to taste with salt and pepper.
5. **Bring the soup back to a boil, stirring constantly. Then remove from heat and cool. When slightly cool, stir in the oysters.**

To freeze: Pour the soup into plastic container leaving room at the top to allow for the expansion of the liquid during the freezing. Seal, label and freeze.

To serve: Put the frozen soup in the top of a double boiler and gently heat over simmering water.

Serves 6-8.

Vegetable Soup

2 medium carrots, chopped	6 cups (1½ liters) beef stock
2 turnips, chopped	1 teaspoon thyme
2 small onions, chopped	2 tablespoons chopped
1 cup chopped celery	parsley
4 teaspoons (20 g) butter	1 bay leaf
2½ tablespoons cornstarch	salt and pepper

1. Saute the carrots, turnips, onions and celery in the butter until the onions are golden brown.
2. Sprinkle on the cornstarch and mix well.
3. Slowly add the stock, stirring constantly.
4. Add the thyme, parsley, bay leaf and salt and pepper to taste. Bring to a boil. Reduce heat, cover and simmer for one hour. Cool.

To freeze: Pour the soup into a plastic container leaving 1 inch (2½ cm) of room at the top to allow for expansion during freezing.

To serve: Reheat frozen soup in a heavy bottomed saucepan over a low heat or in a double boiler over simmering water.

Serves 6.

Chicken Liver Pâté

2½ tablespoons oil
1 medium onion, minced
4 teaspoons plain flour
½ lb (250 g) chicken livers
1 hard boiled egg yolk

1 cup (250 g) butter
2 tablespoons sherry
2½ tablespoons cream
salt and pepper

1. Heat the oil and saute the onion until golden brown. Remove the onion from the frypan.
2. Coat the livers with the flour and cook in the frypan, covered, for 7 minutes, stirring a few times.
3. Chop livers finely and press through a sieve with onion and egg yolk or put livers, onion and egg yolk in an electric blender and puree.
4. Put into a bowl and add the butter, sherry and cream. Season to taste with salt and pepper. Mix well.

To freeze: Put into an aluminum foil container or a plastic container. Seal, label and freeze.

To serve: Thaw at room temperature for about 3 hours.

Quiche Lorraine

shortcrust pastry
½ lb (250 g) bacon
¼ lb (125 g) Swiss cheese
¼ lb (125 g) Cheddar cheese
4 eggs

1½ cups (375 ml) cream
1 teaspoon salt
¼ teaspoon black pepper
pinch of nutmeg

1. Roll out the pastry and line a 9 inch (23-cm) pie tin.
2. Remove the rind from the bacon, cut into small pieces and fry until crisp. Drain and arrange on the bottom of the pie tin.
3. Grate the cheeses and put on top of the bacon.
4. Slightly beat the eggs and mix with the cream, salt, pepper and nutmeg. Pour over the cheese.
5. Bake in a 350°F (180°C) oven for about 40 minutes or until set. Cool.

To freeze: Wrap tightly in aluminum foil. Seal, label and freeze.

To serve: Thaw in refrigerator, covered, for about six hours and serve at room temperature. Or heat in a 350°F (180°C) oven for about 20 minutes after thawing.

Serves 6.

Tuna Fish Pâté

1 can (440 g) tuna fish	5 black peppercorns
milk	3 tablespoons (45 g) butter
1½ tablespoons chopped	2½ tablespoons plain flour
parsley	⅓ cup (85 ml) cream
1 bay leaf	2 teaspoons lemon juice

1. Drain the tuna and using the liquid from the tin, add enough milk to make up 1¼ cups (300 ml).
2. Pour into a saucepan and add the parsley, bay leaf and peppercorns. Bring to a boil. Reduce heat and simmer for 15 minutes. Strain.
3. Melt the butter and stir in the flour. Slowly add the milk mixture, stirring constantly. Cook over a low heat until thickened.
4. Break up the tuna with a fork until there are no large chunks. Add to the sauce with the lemon juice and cream. Cool.

To freeze: Line a container with aluminum foil and pour in the pâté. Cover tightly with another layer of foil. Seal, label and freeze.

To serve: Thaw at room temperature for about two hours. Turn out onto a serving plate and remove all the foil.

Shrimp Cocktail

1½ lb (750 g) peeled, cooked	1½ teaspoons salt
shrimp	½ teaspoon pepper
1 cup (250 g) mayonnaise	½ teaspoon paprika
2½ tablespoons tomato paste	pinch of cayenne
2½ tablespoons lemon juice	dash of Tabasco sauce
2 tablespoons horseradish	lettuce leaves
sauce	chopped chives

1. De-vein the shrimp and quickly rinse under cold running water.
2. Mix together the mayonnaise, tomato paste, lemon juice, horseradish sauce, salt, pepper, paprika, cayenne and Tabasco sauce.
3. Add the shrimp and mix well.

To freeze: Put the Shrimp Cocktail in a plastic container leaving ½ inch (1 cm) of room at the top to allow for expansion. Seal, label and freeze.

To serve: Thaw in container in refrigerator overnight. Serve on lettuce leaves and sprinkle with chopped chives.

Serves 6.

19

Meat

Hints for Freezing Meat

It is always advisable to remove as much fat as possible from the meat before freezing.

Always pad any protrusions with grease-proof paper before wrapping. This will prevent the wrapping from being punctured and allowing air to penetrate.

Put a piece of plastic wrap or aluminum foil between steaks or chops. This makes unpacking easier and thawing quicker.

Cooked meat to be eaten cold should be cut into thin slices and packed with either grease-proof paper or plastic wrap between each slice. They should then be wrapped in aluminum foil with all the air pressed out.

Airtight packaging of meat is very important to prevent dehydration, freezer burn and rancidity.

Chops, steaks and small pieces of meat can be cooked frozen but large cuts and joints should be thawed before cooking.

Be sure to skim off the excess fat from the top of casseroles and stews before freezing.

Cold Roast Fillet of Beef

3 lb (1½ kg) fillet of beef
black pepper
paprika
4 tablespoons (60 g) butter

1. Remove any fat from the beef.
2. Rub in black pepper and paprika.
3. Melt the butter and brush over the meat.
4. Coat a large piece of heavy duty aluminum foil with the remaining melted butter and securely wrap the fillet in it.
5. Cook on a roasting rack in a 475°F (250°C) oven for 15 minutes. Then reduce the heat to 400°F (200°C) and cook for another 15 minutes. Fold the foil back and cook for a further ten minutes. Remove from oven and cool.

To freeze: When cool, slice the beef into thin slices. Put a piece of plastic wrap between each slice, then wrap in a large sheet of plastic. Put in a plastic bag and remove the air either with a vacuum pump, a straw or by submerging in a bowl of water.* Seal tightly, label and freeze.

To serve: Thaw beef in its wrapping overnight in the refrigerator. Serve at room temperature.

Serves 10-12.

*See Hints for Freezing - Sealing and Covering in the front of the book.

Beef Goulash

3 lb (1½ kg) rump steak	1 teaspoon sugar
¼ cup (65 ml) oil	salt and pepper
5 medium onions, sliced	⅔ cup (165 ml) beef stock
1½ tablespoons paprika	2 cloves garlic, minced
1 lb (500 g) tomatoes, chopped	4 tablespoons sour cream

1. Cut the meat into cubes and discard all fat.
2. Heat the oil and brown the meat well on all sides.
3. Add the onions and cook until the onions are transparent.
4. Add the paprika, tomatoes, sugar, salt and pepper to taste and the beef stock. Cover and simmer for one hour. Cool and skim off the fat.

To freeze: Put the goulash into a plastic container. Leave 1 inch (2½ cm) of room at the top to allow for expansion of the liquid during freezing. Cover, seal, label and freeze.

To serve: Thaw overnight in the refrigerator or for five hours at room temperature. Stir in the garlic and heat in a saucepan. Just before serving stir in the sour cream.

Serves 8.

Beef in Beer

1½ lb (750 g) stewing beef	4 teaspoons cornstarch
2½ tablespoons oil	1½ cups (375 ml) beef stock
2 medium onions, sliced	2 tablespoons tomato paste
¼ lb (125 g) small mushrooms	2½ tablespoons chopped parsley
½ lb (250 g) carrots, sliced	1½ cups (375 ml) beer

CONTINUED ON NEXT PAGE

1. Cut the meat into cubes and saute in the oil until brown on all sides. Remove from the pan and put into a casserole.
2. Saute the onions in the same pan until golden brown. Add to the meat with the mushrooms and the carrots.
3. Mix the cornstarch with a little of the stock in the same pan. Then stir in the rest of the stock, the tomato paste and the parsley. Bring to a boil, stirring constantly. Pour over the beef and vegetables.
4. Season to taste with salt and pepper and pour on the beer.
5. Cook, covered, in a 350°F (180°C) oven for 2-3 hours or until the beef is tender. Cool.

To freeze: Put into a plastic container. Seal, label and freeze.

To serve: Thaw overnight in the refrigerator. Put into a casserole dish and reheat in a 350°F (180°C) oven for about one hour. Serves 4.

Beef Stroganoff

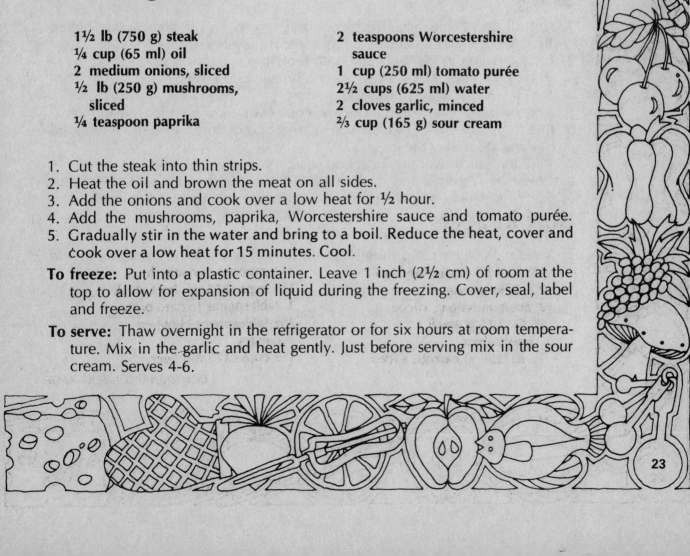

1½ lb (750 g) steak	2 teaspoons Worcestershire
¼ cup (65 ml) oil	sauce
2 medium onions, sliced	1 cup (250 ml) tomato purée
½ lb (250 g) mushrooms,	2½ cups (625 ml) water
sliced	2 cloves garlic, minced
¼ teaspoon paprika	⅔ cup (165 g) sour cream

1. Cut the steak into thin strips.
2. Heat the oil and brown the meat on all sides.
3. Add the onions and cook over a low heat for ½ hour.
4. Add the mushrooms, paprika, Worcestershire sauce and tomato purée.
5. Gradually stir in the water and bring to a boil. Reduce the heat, cover and cook over a low heat for 15 minutes. Cool.

To freeze: Put into a plastic container. Leave 1 inch (2½ cm) of room at the top to allow for expansion of liquid during the freezing. Cover, seal, label and freeze.

To serve: Thaw overnight in the refrigerator or for six hours at room temperature. Mix in the garlic and heat gently. Just before serving mix in the sour cream. Serves 4-6.

Beef Burgundy

2 lb (1 kg) topside steak	1½ tablespoons chopped
4 tablespoons (60 g) butter	parsley
¼ lb (125 g) bacon, chopped	¼ cup (65 ml) brandy
2½ tablespoons plain flour	salt and pepper
1 cup (250 ml) red wine	10 small onions
1 cup (250 ml) beef stock	1½ tablespoons oil
2 bay leaves	2 cloves garlic, crushed

1. Cut the meat into bite-size pieces and brown on all sides in the butter. Remove from the saucepan and put into a casserole dish.
2. Fry the bacon in the saucepan until brown.
3. Add in the flour and, stirring constantly, allow to brown.
4. Slowly add the wine and stock.
5. Add the bay leaves and parsley and cook over a low heat for five minutes.
6. In a separate small saucepan heat the brandy and ignite it. While still flaming, pour over the meat.
7. Pour the sauce over the meat and season well with salt and pepper.
8. Cover the casserole and cook in a 325°F (160°C) oven for about 1½ hours.
9. Saute the whole onions in the oil until brown. Drain and add to the casserole. Cover, reduce the heat to 300°F (150°C) and cook for another hour. Remove from the oven and cool.

To freeze: Pour the Beef Burgundy into a plastic container. Seal, label and freeze.

To serve: Thaw overnight in the refrigerator or for six hours at room temperature. Stir in the garlic and either heat gently on the top of the stove in a saucepan or put into a casserole dish and heat in a 325°F (160°C) oven until hot. Remove the bay leaves before serving.

Serves 6-8.

Fruity Beef with Almonds

10 prunes
1 medium onion, chopped
1 carrot, sliced
4 tablespoons oil
1 cooking apple, chopped
1½ lb (750 g) chuck steak
2½ tablespoons plain flour

1½ teaspoons salt
½ teaspoon pepper
1½ cups (375 ml) beef stock
½ teaspoon paprika
salt and pepper
½ cup (80 g) whole
    blanched almonds

1. Soak the prunes in enough water to cover for two hours. Drain and remove the stones.
2. Saute the onion and carrot in the oil for five minutes.
3. Add the apple and cook for another five minutes. Remove from pan.
4. Cut the steak into cubes and toss in a mixture of the flour, salt and pepper.
5. Brown the meat on all sides in the oil.
6. Return the vegetables and the apple to the pan and mix well.
7. Add the beef stock, the paprika and salt and pepper to taste. Bring to a boil. Reduce heat, cover and cook over a low heat for about two hours. Cool and stir in the prunes.

To freeze: Place in a plastic container leaving about 1 inch (2½ cm) of room at the top to allow for expansion of the liquid during freezing. Cover, seal, label and freeze.

To serve: Thaw overnight in the refrigerator or for six hours at room temperature. Heat through in a saucepan. Just before serving add the almonds and mix well.

Serves 4-6.

Beef and Cheese Loaf

2 lb (1 kg) ground beef	½ lb (250 g) cheese, sliced
2 teaspoons salt	⅔ cup (165 ml) red wine
½ teaspoon pepper	¼ cup (65 ml) tomato purée
½ teaspoon thyme	
2½ tablespoons chopped parsley	

1. Mix together the ground beef, salt, pepper, thyme and parsley.
2. Divide the mixture in half and press one half into the bottom of a loaf tin.
3. Place the sliced cheese on top of the meat, then cover with the other half of the meat mixture.
4. Mix together the wine and tomato purée and pour over the loaf.
5. Bake in a 350°F (180°C) oven for 30 minutes. Cool.

To freeze: Cover the tin and seal. Label and freeze.

To serve: Thaw overnight in the refrigerator or for six hours at room temperature. Bake in a 350°F (180°C) oven for 45 minutes.

Serves 4-6.

Beef and Beans

2 medium onions, chopped	1 can (250 g) baked beans
2½ tablespoons oil	4 teaspoons chilli sauce
1 lb (500 g) ground beef	1½ teaspoons salt
2 tomatoes, chopped	½ teaspoon pepper

1. Saute the onions in the oil until golden brown.
2. Add the meat and cook until well browned, stirring constantly to break up the meat.
3. Add the tomatoes and cook for five minutes.
4. Stir in the beans, chilli sauce, salt and pepper. Cover and cook for ten minutes. Remove from heat and cool.

To freeze: Put into a plastic container and cover. Seal, label and freeze.

To serve: Thaw overnight in the refrigerator or for six hours at room temperature. Put into a saucepan and gently heat for 20 minutes.

Serves 4.

Liver Casserole

1½ lb (750 g) lamb's liver
2 tablespoons plain flour
1½ teaspoons salt
½ teaspoon pepper

3 medium onions *
2½ tablespoons oil
1 cup (250 ml) beef stock
1 bay leaf

1. Cover the liver with warm water and allow to soak for ½ hour. Drain and dry.
2. Mix together the flour, salt and pepper. Coat the liver in the flour mixture.
3. Saute the onions in the oil until transparent. Remove from pan.
4. Brown the liver on both sides over a high heat.
5. Reduce the heat and return the onions to the pan.
6. Add the beef stock, bay leaf and any leftover flour. Mix well.
7. Cover and cook over a low heat for about one hour. Cool.

To freeze: Put into an airtight container. Cover, seal, label and freeze.

To serve: Thaw overnight in the refrigerator or for six hours at room temperature. Put into a saucepan and heat gently for about ½ hour. Serves 4-6.

Beef and Macaroni

2 lb (1 kg) round steak
1 teaspoon salt
½ teaspoon pepper
3 tablespoons (45 g) butter
½ cup (125 g) tomato paste
4 teaspoons lemon juice
½ teaspoon sugar

1 medium carrot, sliced
⅔ cup (165 ml) water
1 clove garlic, minced
½ lb (250 g) macaroni
grated Parmesan cheese
chopped parsley

1. Cut the meat into cubes and sprinkle with salt and pepper.
2. Melt the butter in a saucepan and brown the meat on all sides.
3. Mix together tomato paste, lemon juice, sugar, carrot and water. Pour over the meat and bring to boil. Reduce heat, cover and cook over a low heat for 2-3 hours or until tender. Add more water if necessary. Cool.

To freeze: Put into an aluminum container, cover, seal, label and freeze.

To serve: Thaw overnight in the refrigerator or for six hours at room temperature. Mix in the garlic. Bake in a 180°C (350°F) oven until heated through. While beef is heating, boil macaroni in boiling salted water until tender. Drain and put on a serving dish. Pour meat over macaroni. Sprinkle with Parmesan cheese and parsley and serve. Serves 4-6.

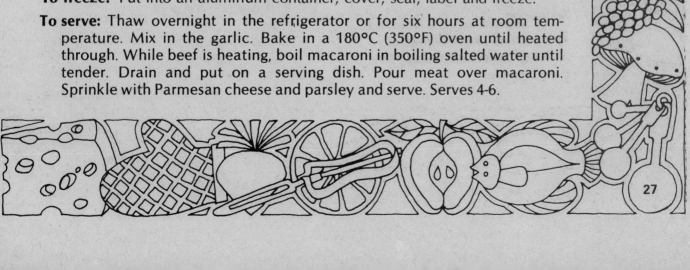

27

Stuffed Lamb Casserole

1 shoulder of lamb (2 kg)	1 medium carrot, sliced
2 cups dried bread crumbs	1 medium onion, sliced
½ lb (250 g) sausage meat	¼ lb (125 g) small mushrooms
12 green olives, pitted and chopped	1 teaspoon rosemary
salt and pepper	1 teaspoon crushed bay leaves
1½ teaspoons grated lemon rind	3 cups (750 ml) lamb stock
	2 slices bacon, chopped

1. Remove the bone from the lamb.
2. Mix together the bread crumbs, sausage meat, olives, salt and pepper to taste and the lemon rind.
3. Spread the stuffing on the lamb and roll up. Secure with string.
4. Put the meat in a frypan and brown on all sides. Put into a casserole dish.
5. Add the carrot, onion, mushrooms, rosemary, crushed bay leaves, stock and bacon.
6. Cover and cook in a 350°F (180°C) oven for two hours. During the cooking time turn the lamb over several times. When cooked, remove from the oven and cool.

To freeze: Put the lamb and the liquid in a plastic container. Leave about 1 inch (2½ cm) of room at the top to allow for expansion of the liquid during freezing. Seal, label and freeze.

To serve: Thaw overnight in the refrigerator or for six hours at room temperature. Return to a casserole dish and heat in a 325°F (160°C) oven for one hour.

Serves 6.

Lamb in Cider

2 lb (1 kg) stewing lamb	½ cup (125 ml) lamb stock
plain flour	⅔ cup (165 ml) cider
salt and pepper	4 teaspoons Worcestershire sauce
3 tablespoons (45 g) butter	salt and pepper
2 small onions, chopped	
2½ tablespoons chopped parsley	

CONTINUED ON OPPOSITE PAGE

1. Cut the meat into bite-size cubes.
2. Season the flour with salt and pepper and toss the lamb cubes in it.
3. Melt the butter and brown the lamb on all sides. Remove the lamb to a casserole dish.
4. Saute the onions in the pan for two minutes. Add to the lamb with the parsley.
5. Heat the stock with the cider, Worcestershire sauce and salt and pepper to taste.
6. Pour over the meat, cover and cook in a 325°F (160°C) oven for about one hour. Cool.

To freeze: Put in a plastic container and cover. Seal, label and freeze.

To serve: Thaw overnight in the refrigerator or for six hours at room temperature. Put into a casserole dish and heat in a 350°F (180°C) oven for 40 minutes.

Serves 6.

Country Stew

1½ lb (750 g) chuck steak	½ cup (125 ml) red wine
1½ teaspoons salt	1 cup (250 ml) water
½ teaspoon pepper	1 green pepper, chopped
2½ tablespoons plain flour	1 carrot, sliced
3 medium onions, chopped	1 parsnip, sliced
4 tablespoons oil	2 cloves garlic, minced
4 tablespoons tomato paste	

1. Cut the steak into cubes, removing all the fat.
2. Mix together the salt, pepper and flour and coat the meat.
3. Saute the onions in the oil until golden brown.
4. Add the meat and brown on all sides.
5. Stir in the tomato paste, red wine, water, green pepper, carrot and parsnip. Season to taste with salt and pepper. Cover and simmer for about two hours or until the meat is tender. Cool.

To freeze: Put into a plastic container. Leave room at the top to allow for expansion of the liquid during freezing. Cover, seal, label and freeze.

To serve: Thaw overnight in the refrigerator or for six hours at room temperature. Mix in the garlic and heat gently in a saucepan.

Serves 4-6.

Kidneys in Red Wine

4 tablespoons (60 g) butter	4 teaspoons tomato paste
2 small onions, chopped	1 teaspoon salt
10 sheep's kidneys	¼ teaspoon black pepper
4 tablespoons plain flour	¼ lb (125 g) small mushrooms
⅔ cup (165 ml) red wine	⅔ cup (110 g) raisins
½ cup (125 ml) beef stock	2½ tablespoons chopped
1 bouquet garni	chives

1. Saute the onions in the butter until golden brown.
2. Remove the core from the kidneys and cut into bite-size pieces.
3. Add the kidneys to the onions and cook over a medium heat for five minutes, stirring constantly.
4. Sprinkle on the flour and mix well.
5. Slowly pour on the wine and beef stock, stirring constantly. Bring to a boil.
6. Add the bouquet garni, tomato paste, salt and pepper. Reduce the heat and simmer for five minutes.
7. Add the mushrooms and raisins and cook for ten minutes.
8. Remove from heat and cool. Remove the bouquet garni.

To freeze: Put into a plastic container. Cover, seal, label and freeze.

To serve: Thaw in container overnight or for six hours at room temperature. Put in a casserole dish and heat in a 325°F (160°C) oven until hot or gently heat in a saucepan on the top of the stove. Garnish with chopped chives.

Serves 4-6.

Lancashire Hotpot

8 best neck chops
2 lamb kidneys
½ lb (250 g) onions, sliced
1 lb (500 g) potatoes, sliced
2½ tablespoons chopped
     parsley

salt and pepper
1½ cups (375 ml) stock
2 tablespoons lard

1. Remove any fat from the chops. Put into a casserole.
2. Chop the kidneys and put into the casserole with the chops.
3. Spread the onions on top and then lay the potato slices on the onions.
4. Sprinkle on the chopped parsley and season well with salt and pepper.
5. Pour in the stock.
6. Melt the lard and brush on the potatoes.
7. Cover and cook in a 375°F (190°C) oven for one hour. Remove the cover and cook for another ½ hour. Cool.

To freeze: Put the hotpot in a plastic container. Seal, label and freeze.

To serve: Thaw overnight in the refrigerator or for six hours at room temperature. Put into a casserole dish and heat in a 325°F (160°C) oven.

Serves 4.

Italian Veal

2 lb (1 kg) veal steak
3 cups dried bread crumbs
1½ tablespoons minced parsley
2½ tablespoons grated
     Parmesan cheese

3 eggs, beaten
oil for frying
salt and pepper
4 cups (1 liter) white sauce
1 lb (500 g) Mozzarella cheese

1. Pound the veal steaks until very thin.
2. Mix together the bread crumbs, parsley and Parmesan cheese.
3. Dip the steaks into the bread crumb mixture, then into the beaten eggs, then again into the bread crumbs.
4. Cook the veal in the oil until brown.
5. Put a layer of the veal into a casserole dish. Sprinkle with salt and pepper. Pour on the white sauce then the sliced cheese. Continue to layer until all the ingredients are used. End with a layer of white sauce. Cool.

To freeze: Cover and seal. Label and freeze.

To serve: Thaw at room temperature for two hours. Bake in a 350°F (180°C) oven for about 40 minutes.

Serves 6.

Veal Marengo

2 lb (1 kg) shoulder of veal	1 cup (250 ml) chicken stock
2½ tablespoons plain flour	1 cup (250 ml) white wine
1 teaspoon salt	1 bay leaf
1 teaspoon pepper	¼ teaspoon thyme
¼ cup (65 ml) oil	salt and pepper
2 medium onions, chopped	¼ lb (125 g) small mushrooms
4 tablespoons tomato paste	2 cloves garlic, minced

1. Cut the veal into cubes, discarding any fat.
2. Mix the flour with the salt and pepper. Toss the veal cubes in the flour.
3. Heat the oil and brown the meat well.
4. Add the onions and cook for five minutes over a medium heat.
5. Stir in the tomato paste, chicken stock and white wine. Cook for another five minutes.
6. Add the bay leaf, thyme, salt and pepper to taste and cook, covered, for one hour.
7. Add the mushrooms and cook for another ten minutes. Cool.

To freeze: Put into a plastic container. Allow ½ inch (1 cm) of room at the top to allow for expansion of the liquid during freezing. Cover, seal, label and freeze.

To serve: Thaw overnight in the refrigerator or for six hours at room temperature. When completely thawed, stir in the garlic and heat through in a saucepan or in a casserole dish in a 350°F (180°C) oven.

Serves 6.

Veal and Chicken Curry

1 lb (500 g) veal steak	4 teaspoons curry powder
3 chicken breasts	2 teaspoons salt
½ cup plain flour	¼ teaspoon ginger
salt and pepper	¼ teaspoon dry mustard
⅓ cup (85 ml) oil	2½ tablespoons plain flour
2 medium onions, chopped	2½ cups (625 ml) chicken stock
1 cooking apple, peeled, cored and chopped	½ cup (125 ml) cream

1. Cut the veal into cubes. Remove the chicken meat from the skin and bones and cut into cubes.
2. Mix the flour with salt and pepper to taste and mix with the veal and chicken.
3. Heat the oil in a frypan and add the coated meat. Cook until browned on all sides. Remove from frypan and keep warm in a large saucepan.
4. Saute the onions in the oil remaining in the frypan (add more oil if necessary) until transparent. Add the apple and cook for three minutes.
5. Stir in the curry powder, salt, ginger, mustard and the 2½ tablespoons flour.
6. Slowly add the stock, stirring constantly. Bring to a boil.
7. Pour the curry sauce over the chicken and veal.
8. Add the cream and mix well.
9. Cook over low heat for about ½ hour. Cool quickly by putting saucepan into ice water.

To freeze: Pour into a plastic container allowing space at the top for expansion of the liquid during freezing. Seal, label and freeze.

To serve: Allow to thaw for about 3 hours at room temperature. Put into casserole dish and heat in a 350°F (180°C) oven for about 1½ hours or until heated through.

Serves 6.

N.B. Because curry and onions develop undesirable flavours over a long period, it is advisable not to store for more than one month.

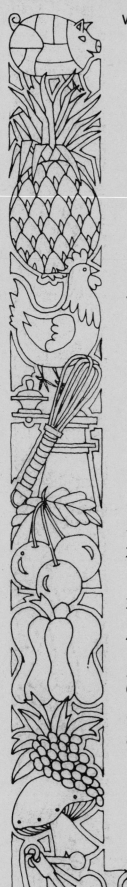

Veal Casserole

1½ lb (750 g) stewing veal
¼ lb (125 g) bacon, chopped
4 tablespoons (60 g) butter
2 carrots, sliced
2 onions, chopped
½ cup chopped celery
1½ tablespoons chopped parsley
½ cup plain flour

2½ cups (625 ml) chicken stock
4 teaspoons tomato paste
1½ tablespoons sherry
2 teaspoons Worcestershire sauce
1 teaspoon grated lemon rind
salt and pepper

1. Cut the veal into cubes removing any fat.
2. Put the meat, bacon and one tablespoon of butter into a saucepan and cook until the meat is well browned. Remove the veal and bacon from the pan to a casserole dish but leave the drippings.
3. Saute the carrots, onions, celery and parsley in the drippings until the onions are golden brown. Add to the meat in the casserole dish.
4. Melt the remaining butter in the saucepan and stir in the flour. Cook until brown.
5. Slowly add the chicken stock, stirring constantly. Cook until thick.
6. Add the tomato paste, sherry, Worcestershire sauce and grated lemon rind. Season to taste with salt and pepper.
7. Pour into the casserole with the meat and vegetable and mix well.
8. Cook in a 325°F (160°C) oven for about two hours. Cool.

To freeze: Put into a plastic container. Cover, seal, label and freeze.

To serve: Thaw in the refrigerator overnight, or at room temperature for 6 hours. Return to a casserole dish and heat in a 325°F (160°C) oven for about 45 minutes.

Serves 4.

Veal Paprika

2½ tablespoons oil	2 teaspoons salt
2 medium onions, chopped	½ teaspoon pepper
2 lb (1 kg) ground veal	1 clove garlic, minced
2½ tablespoons plain flour	½ cup (125 g) sour cream
2½ tablespoons paprika	4 tablespoons grated cheese
1 cup (250 ml) water	
1 lb (500 g) tomatoes, chopped	

1. Heat the oil and saute the onions until golden brown.
2. Add the meat and cook, stirring constantly to break up the meat, until meat is well browned.
3. Sprinkle on the flour and paprika and mix well.
4. Stir in the water and the tomatoes. Add salt and pepper and mix well.
5. Cover and simmer for about one hour.

To freeze: Put into a plastic container and cover. Seal, label and freeze.

To serve: Thaw overnight in the refrigerator or for six hours at room temperature. Mix in the garlic and put into a casserole dish. Heat in a 350°F (180°C) oven for ½ hour. Stir in the sour cream and sprinkle with the grated cheese. Return to the oven until the cheese melts.

Serves 4-6.

Easy Veal

    3 tablespoons (45 g) butter
    1½ lb (750 g) veal steak
    1 can (470 g) tomato soup
    1 cup (125 g) grated Cheddar
      cheese
    salt and pepper

1. Melt the butter and brown the veal steaks on both sides. Put into a freezer-to-oven dish and pour any dripping from the pan over the meat.
2. Heat together the soup, cheese and salt and pepper to taste. Pour over the veal.
3. Cover and bake in a 350°F (180°C) oven for ½ hour. Cool.

To freeze: Cover the dish, seal, label and freeze.

To serve: Thaw overnight in the refrigerator or for six hours at room temperature. Cook for 45 minutes in a 325°F (160°C) oven, covered.

Serves 6.

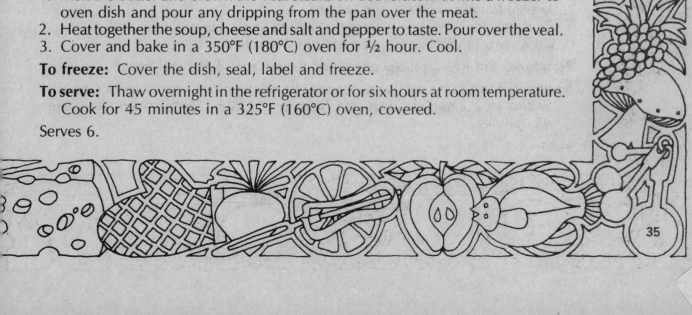

Veal and Pork Meatballs

1 lb (500 g) ground veal
½ lb (250 g) ground pork
1 cup (60 g) fresh bread crumbs
1 medium onion, minced
2½ tablespoons chopped parsley
1½ teaspoons salt
1 teaspoon pepper

1 egg, beaten
4 tablespoons (60 g) butter
1 cup (250 ml) white wine
2 tablespoons plain flour
1½ teaspoons crushed bay leaves
1 lb (500 g) tomatoes, chopped

1. Combine the veal, pork, bread crumbs, onion, parsley, salt and pepper. Mix well.
2. Add the beaten egg and form into small balls. Put into the refrigerator for about ½ hour.
3. Melt the butter in a saucepan, add the meatballs and cook over a medium heat until well browned on all sides. Remove from saucepan.
4. Mix together a little of the white wine with the flour, then add the rest of the wine. Pour into the saucepan and bring to a boil, stirring constantly. Reduce heat and cook until thickened.
5. Add the crushed bay leaves and tomatoes and mix well. Cook for ten minutes.
6. Return the meatballs to the saucepan. Cover and cook for another five minutes. Remove from heat and cool.

To freeze: Put into an airtight container. Seal, label and freeze.

To serve: Thaw overnight in the refrigerator or for six hours at room temperature. Put into a saucepan and gently heat for about 20 minutes.

Serves 4.

Pork Chops with Pineapple

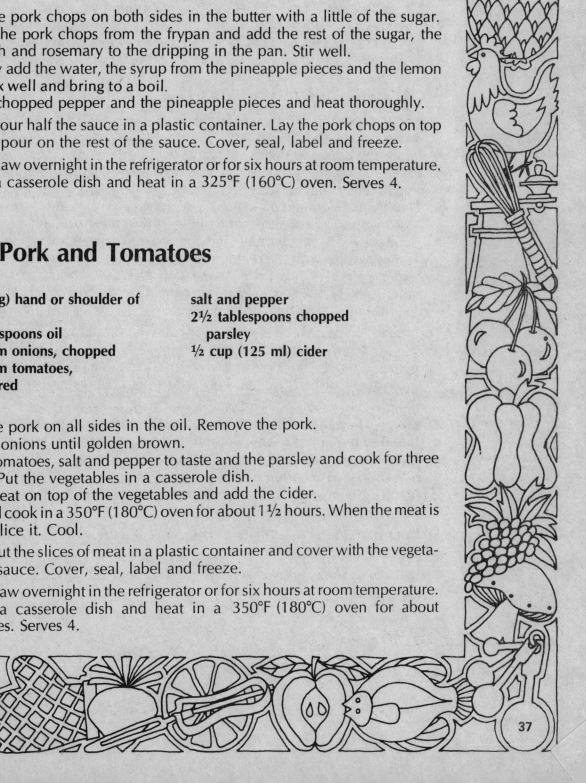

4 pork chops	1½ cups (375 ml) water
2 tablespoons butter	1 can (440 g) pineapple pieces
2½ tablespoons brown sugar	2½ tablespoons lemon juice
4 teaspoons cornstarch	1 green pepper, chopped
½ teaspoon rosemary	

1. Brown the pork chops on both sides in the butter with a little of the sugar.
2. Remove the pork chops from the frypan and add the rest of the sugar, the cornstarch and rosemary to the dripping in the pan. Stir well.
3. Gradually add the water, the syrup from the pineapple pieces and the lemon juice. Mix well and bring to a boil.
4. Add the chopped pepper and the pineapple pieces and heat thoroughly.

To freeze: Pour half the sauce in a plastic container. Lay the pork chops on top and then pour on the rest of the sauce. Cover, seal, label and freeze.

To serve: Thaw overnight in the refrigerator or for six hours at room temperature. Put into a casserole dish and heat in a 325°F (160°C) oven. Serves 4.

Braised Pork and Tomatoes

2 lb (1 kg) hand or shoulder of pork	salt and pepper
2½ tablespoons oil	2½ tablespoons chopped parsley
2 medium onions, chopped	½ cup (125 ml) cider
8 medium tomatoes, quartered	

1. Brown the pork on all sides in the oil. Remove the pork.
2. Saute the onions until golden brown.
3. Add the tomatoes, salt and pepper to taste and the parsley and cook for three minutes. Put the vegetables in a casserole dish.
4. Put the meat on top of the vegetables and add the cider.
5. Cover and cook in a 350°F (180°C) oven for about 1½ hours. When the meat is cooked, slice it. Cool.

To freeze: Put the slices of meat in a plastic container and cover with the vegetables and sauce. Cover, seal, label and freeze.

To serve: Thaw overnight in the refrigerator or for six hours at room temperature. Put into a casserole dish and heat in a 350°F (180°C) oven for about 45 minutes. Serves 4.

Sweet and Sour Pork

2 lb (1 kg) fillet of pork	¼ lb (125 g) blanched carrots
2½ tablespoons soy sauce	½ cup (125 ml) oil
4 teaspoons sherry	2½ tablespoons sherry
plain flour	2½ tablespoons lemon juice
½ cup (125 ml) oil	¼ cup (65 ml) tomato sauce
2 green peppers	2½ tablespoons soy sauce
1 red pepper	½ cup brown sugar
2 medium onions	1½ cups pineapple cubes
¼ lb (125 g) blanched green beans	4 teaspoons plain flour
	1 cup (250 ml) water

1. Cut the pork into cubes.
2. Mix together the soy sauce and sherry and stir in the pork. Allow to marinate for ½ hour.
3. Drain the pork and coat with flour.
4. Heat the oil and fry the pork pieces until brown, stirring often. Remove from frypan and drain on absorbent paper.
5. Slice the peppers and the onions. Cut the green beans and carrots into strips.
6. Mix together the vegetables and saute in the ½ cup hot oil for about 7 minutes.
7. Combine the sherry, lemon juice, tomato sauce, soy sauce and sugar. Stir into the vegetables with the pineapple cubes. Bring to a boil.
8. Mix the flour with a little of the cup of water, then add the remaining water. Slowly add to the vegetable mixture, stirring constantly. Bring to a boil. Remove from heat and cool.

To freeze: Place the cubes of pork on a tray and put in the freezer uncovered. When frozen put in a plastic bag, remove air and seal. Label and return to freezer. Pour the cold sweet and sour sauce into a plastic container allowing room at the top for the expansion of the liquid during freezing. Seal, label and freeze.

To serve: Thaw the sauce for 5 hours and the pork for 2 hours at room temperature. Fry the pork in some oil until brown and tender. Drain and place in a serving dish. Bring the sauce to a boil and immediately pour over the pork. Serve with boiled rice.

Serves 6-8.

Orange Pork Chops

6 large pork chops
plain flour
salt and pepper
2½ tablespoons oil

2 medium onions, sliced
2½ tablespoons vinegar
1½ cups (375 ml) orange juice
2 tablespoons brown sugar

1. Dredge the pork chops in flour seasoned well with salt and pepper.
2. Brown the chops in the hot oil on both sides. Remove the chops from the pan.
3. Saute the onions in the same pan until transparent.
4. Return the chops to the pan and add the vinegar, orange juice and sugar. Mix well.
5. Simmer gently until the chops are tender. Cool.

To freeze: Put into a plastic container. Cover, seal, label and freeze.

To serve: Thaw overnight in the refrigerator or for six hours at room temperature. Put into a casserole dish and heat in a 350°F (180°C) oven for about 40 minutes. Serves 6.

Lamb Cutlets

1 medium onion, chopped
3 tablespoons (45 g) butter
8 lamb cutlets
1 lb (500 g) tomatoes, chopped
2½ tablespoons chopped mint

2 ½ tablespoons tomato paste
2 tablespoons malt vinegar
2 teaspoons sugar
1½ teaspoons salt
½ teaspoon pepper

1. Saute the onion in the butter until transparent. Remove from pan.
2. Brown the cutlets on both sides in the same pan. Remove.
3. Put the chopped tomatoes in the pan (add more butter if necessary) and cook over a medium heat for three minutes.
4. Mash the tomatoes with the mint, tomato paste, vinegar, sugar, salt and pepper. Stirring constantly, cook for three minutes.
5. Return cutlets and onion to the pan, cover and cook 15 minutes. Cool.

To freeze: Place in an airtight container. Cover, seal, label and freeze.

To serve: Thaw overnight in the refrigerator or for six hours at room temperature. Put into a saucepan, cover and gently heat for 20 minutes. Serves 4.

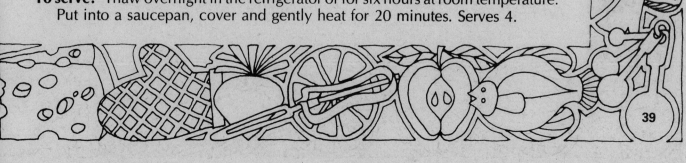

Devilled Pork Chops

3 teaspoons curry powder	½ teaspoon pepper
2 teaspoons mustard powder	½ cup (125 ml) chicken stock
8 pork chops	1 cup (250 ml) white wine
4 tablespoons oil	2½ tablespoons cornstarch
2 medium onions, chopped	½ cup (125 ml) milk
2½ tablespoons plain flour	2½ tablespoons white wine
1½ teaspoons salt	vinegar

1. Mix together the curry powder and mustard powder. Pierce the pork chops with a fork and rub in the powder mixture on both sides of the chops. Set aside for 45 minutes.
2. Heat the oil and saute the onions until golden brown.
3. Coat the chops in a mixture of the flour, salt and pepper.
4. Add to the onions and brown.
5. Add the chicken stock and white wine and bring to a boil. Reduce heat, cover and simmer for one hour.
6. Mix the cornstarch with the milk and stir into the sauce. Cook until sauce is thick.
7. Remove from heat and stir in the vinegar. Cool.

To freeze: Put the chops into a plastic container and pour the sauce over the top. Cover, seal, label and freeze.

To serve: Thaw overnight in the refrigerator or for six hours at room temperature. Put into a casserole dish and cook in a 350°F (180°C) oven for about ½ hour.

Serves 4.

Chicken

Hints for Poultry

When freezing raw poultry, clean and prepare the bird as if for cooking.

Always tie the legs together and tie the wings close to the body. Wrap any protrusions with waxed paper before wrapping with heavy duty aluminum foil.

Raw poultry should be thawed in its wrapping in the refrigerator.

It is not necessary to thaw casseroles. They may be put directly into a 350°F (180°C) oven for about 45 minutes to one hour.

A 5 lb (2½ kg) bird will thaw overnight in the refrigerator. It will take about 36 hours to thaw a bird from 5 lb (2½ kg) to 10 lb (5 kg).

Chicken Tettrazini

1½ lb (750 g) cooked chicken meat	2½ cups (625 ml) chicken stock
¾ lb (375 g) spaghetti	2½ cups (625 ml) milk
½ lb (250 g) small mushrooms	salt and pepper
¾ cup (185 g) butter	½ cup (125 ml) white wine
7 tablespoons plain flour	1 cup grated cheese

1. Cut the chicken into bite-size pieces.
2. Cook the spaghetti in boiling salted water until just tender. Drain thoroughly and then cover with boiling water to keep the strands separate.
3. Saute the mushrooms in half the butter for five minutes. Remove from heat.
4. In a separate saucepan, melt the remainder of the butter. Add the flour and, stirring constantly, cook for one minute. Remove from heat.
5. Continuing to stir, gradually add the stock and the milk. Return to the heat and bring to a boil. Reduce heat and cook for two minutes, stirring constantly.
6. Season to taste with salt and pepper. Remove from heat.
7. Stir in the wine and cheese.
8. Mix half the sauce with the chicken and the other half with the drained spaghetti and the mushrooms. Cool.

To freeze: Line a shallow oven-proof dish with enough aluminum foil to cover the top. Pour in the spaghetti mixture first, then the chicken mixture. Cover with the foil and freeze until solid. When frozen, remove from the dish and put the foil-wrapped chicken tettrazini in a plastic bag. Seal, label and return to the freezer.

To serve: Remove wrapping and put into the dish in which it was originally frozen. Heat in a 350°F (180°C) oven for one hour. Gently mix a few times during the heating.

Serves 6.

Chicken Chablis

1 lb (500 g) cooked chicken meat	1 cup grated cheese
4 tablespoons (60 g) butter	2½ tablespoons chopped parsley
5 tablespoons plain flour	salt and pepper
2 cups (500 ml) milk	4 medium tomatoes, sliced
⅔ cup (165 ml) Chablis	

1. Cut the chicken into bite-size pieces.
2. Melt the butter in a saucepan and add the flour. Mix well and cook for two minutes over a low heat.
3. Slowly add the milk and, stirring constantly, bring to a boil. Reduce heat and cook for three minutes.
4. Remove the white sauce from the heat and add the wine, half the cheese, the parsley and salt and pepper to taste.
5. Put the chicken into a shallow baking dish and pour the sauce on top.
6. Arrange the slices of tomatoes over the sauce and sprinkle with the remaining cheese.

To freeze: Cover with aluminum foil. Seal, label and freeze.

To serve: Loosen the wrapping and heat the frozen chicken in a 350°F (180°C) oven for one hour. Remove the foil and cook for another 45 minutes.

Serves 4.

43

Hong Kong Chicken

1 lb (500 g) cooked chicken
   meat
½ cup chopped celery
3 medium onions, sliced
1½ teaspoons salt
½ teaspoon pepper
4 teaspoons brown sugar
5 cups (1¼ liters) chicken
   stock

½ lb (250 g) bean sprouts
1 can (235 g) bamboo shoots
4 tablespoons cornstarch
4 tablespoons soy sauce
¼ lb (125 g) mushrooms,
   sliced

1. Cut the chicken meat into strips.
2. Put the celery, onions, salt, pepper, sugar and chicken stock in a saucepan and bring to a boil. Reduce heat, cover and simmer for 20 minutes.
3. Add the chicken strips, bean sprouts, bamboo shoots and the cornstarch mixed with the soy sauce and a little water. Mix well and cook for five minutes.
4. Add the mushrooms and cook for another five minutes. Cool.

To freeze: Put into a plastic container leaving about 1 inch (2½ cm) of room at the top to allow for expansion of the liquid during the freezing. Cover, seal, label and freeze.

To serve: Thaw overnight in the refrigerator or for six hours at room temperature. Put into a saucepan, cover and heat gently for 20 minutes.

Serves 4.

Indonesian Chicken

1 chicken (1½ kg - 3 lb)	1½ tablespoons desiccated
2½ tablespoons peanut butter	coconut
2 medium onions, chopped	2 tablespoons soy sauce
⅔ cup (105 g) peanuts	1½ teaspoons salt
4 teaspoons oil	1 teaspoon pepper

1. Combine the peanut butter, onions, peanuts, oil, coconut and soy sauce in a saucepan. Mix well and cook over a medium heat for ten minutes.
2. Stuff the chicken with this mixture.
3. Rub the salt and pepper on the chicken.
4. Bake in a 350°F (180°C) oven for about 1½ hours. Cool.

To freeze: Wrap the chicken in aluminum foil. Seal, label and freeze.

To serve: Thaw overnight in the refrigerator or for six hours at room temperature. Serve cold. Or put into a 350°F (180°C) oven and cook for ½ hour.

Serves 4.

Chicken Paprika

3 lb (1½ kg) chicken pieces	3 teaspoons paprika
½ cup plain flour	4 teaspoons tomato paste
salt and pepper	2 cups (500 ml) chicken stock
1 lb (500 g) onions, sliced	salt and pepper
¾ cup (185 g) butter	1 cup (250 g) sour cream

1. Coat the chicken pieces in the flour seasoned with salt and pepper.
2. Saute the onions in half the butter until golden brown. Remove the onions from the pan.
3. Melt the rest of the butter in the pan and brown the chicken pieces on all sides.
4. Return the onions to the pan and add the paprika and tomato paste.
5. Sprinkle on the left-over flour. Mix well.
6. Slowly pour on the chicken stock. Season to taste with salt and pepper and bring to a boil. Put the chicken and the sauce into a casserole dish.
7. Cover and cook in a 325°F (160°C) oven for about one hour. Cool.

To freeze: Put into a plastic container. Cover, seal, label and freeze.

To serve: Heat from frozen in a casserole dish, lightly covered, in a 375°F (190°C) oven for about one hour. Before serving, stir in the sour cream. Reheat, if necessary.

Serves 4-6.

Chicken and Lemon Pie

2½ cups (625 ml) milk
strips of rind of one lemon
4 tablespoons (60 g) butter
5 tablespoons plain flour
1 cup (250 ml) chicken stock
½ teaspoon sugar

salt and pepper
4 tablespoons lemon juice
1 lb (500 g) cooked chicken
meat
1 can (440 g) corn kernels
½ lb (250 g) shortcrust pastry

1. Mix milk and lemon rind in a saucepan and gently heat for ten minutes. Remove the lemon rind and cool the milk.
2. In a separate saucepan, melt the butter and stir in the flour. Stirring constantly, cook over a low heat for one minute. Continuing to stir, gradually add the milk and the stock. Cook until thickened.
3. Add sugar, salt and pepper to taste and lemon juice. Mix well. Remove from heat, cover and cool.
4. Cut the chicken meat into bite-size pieces.
5. Drain the corn and add to the chicken. Spoon into a pie dish.
6. Pour the lemon sauce over the chicken and cover with rolled out pastry.

To freeze: Put into the freezer uncovered. When frozen, wrap well in aluminum foil or in a plastic bag. Seal, label and return to the freezer.

To serve: Remove all the wrapping and thaw, loosely covered in a plastic bag, in the refrigerator overnight or for at least 10 hours. Put the pie on a baking tray and cook in a 400°F (200°C) for about 45 minutes. (Cut a whole in the center of the pastry half-way through the cooking time.)

Serves 4-6.

Chicken Crumble Pie

6 oz (185 g) shortcrust pastry	1½ (375 ml) white sauce
1 lb (500 g) cooked chicken	¼ teaspoon thyme
2½ tablespoons capers	salt and pepper
1½ tablespoons chopped parsley	¾ cup fresh bread crumbs

1. Roll out the pastry and line the bottom of a foil pie dish. Bake the pastry in a 375°F (190°C) oven for 15 minutes.
2. Chop the chicken into small pieces.
3. Mix the chicken with the capers and parsley and add to the white sauce. Heat thoroughly.
4. Add the thyme and salt and pepper to taste.
5. Cool, then pour into the cooked pastry shell. Sprinkle with the bread crumbs.

To freeze: Cover the pie with aluminum foil. Seal, label and freeze.

To serve: Thaw overnight in the refrigerator or for three hours at room temperature. Remove the aluminum foil and heat in a 350°F (180°C) oven until golden brown and heated through.

Serves 4.

Chicken and Rice

2 medium onions, chopped	¼ teaspoon rosemary
5 tablespoons (75 g) butter	2½ tablespoons chopped parsley
1 cup (210 g) rice	1 lb (500 g) cooked chicken meat
2½ cups (625 ml) chicken stock	
salt and pepper	

1. Saute the onions in the butter until golden brown.
2. Mix in the rice and cook until the rice is brown.
3. Add the stock, salt and pepper to taste and the rosemary. Bring to a boil and cook for ten minutes.
4. Cut the chicken into bite-size pieces and add to the rice.
5. Cook over a low heat until all the liquid has been absorbed. Cool.

To freeze: Put into a plastic container. Cover, seal, label and freeze.

To serve: Thaw overnight in the refrigerator or for six hours at room temperature. Put into a saucepan with one cup (250 ml) water and gently heat.

Serves 4-6.

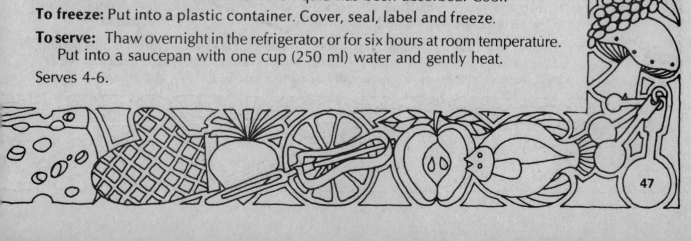

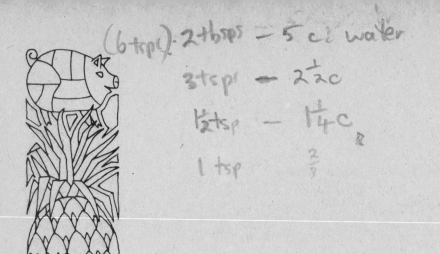

(6 tsp) 2 tbsps = 5 c? water

3 tsp — $2\frac{1}{2}$c

$1\frac{1}{2}$tsp — $1\frac{1}{4}$c

1 tsp $\frac{2}{3}$

Fish and Seafood

Hints for Fish and Seafood

Fish: Small fish may be frozen whole but larger ones should be cut into steaks or fillets. Pieces of fish should be separated with pieces of plastic wrap or foil before wrapping and freezing. Fatty fish such as tuna and salmon should be dipped into a solution of two tablespoons of ascorbic acid to five cups (1¼ liters) water for ½ minute. Drain. Put into plastic bags, seal, label and freeze.

Shrimp: Remove heads but not shells. Rinse in a solution of one teaspoon salt to five cups (1¼ litres) water. Drain and pack in plastic bags or containers. Seal, label and freeze.

Oysters: Remove oysters from shells and thoroughly wash in a solution of one tablespoon of salt to five cups (1¼ liters) water. Drain. Pack in plastic containers and cover with reserved juices. Leave ½ inch (one cm) of space at the top of the container to allow for expansion of liquid during freezing. Cover, seal, label and freeze.

Lobsters and Crabs: If bought alive, they should be cooked by plunging into boiling salted water. Then cool. Remove the meat from the shells and claws and pack into plastic bags, waxed containers or aluminum foil containers. Seal, label and freeze.

Fish with Mushrooms

1½ lb (750 g) fish fillets
4 tablespoons (60 g) butter
¼ lb (125 g) fresh mushrooms
½ cup (125 ml) fish stock
½ cup (125 ml) white wine
1½ tablespoons chopped
    parsley

1½ tablespoons capers
1 teaspoon salt
½ teaspoon pepper
4 teaspoons cornstarch
¼ cup (65 ml) water
½ cup (125 ml) milk

1. Cook the fish in two tablespoons of butter for about three minutes on each side. Remove and keep warm.
2. Melt the remaining tablespoon of butter and saute the sliced mushrooms for two minutes.
3. Stir in the fish stock, white wine, parsley, capers, salt and pepper. Cook for five minutes.
4. Mix the cornstarch with the water and slowly add to the mushroom mixture, stirring constantly. Cook until the sauce is thick.
5. Return the fish to the pan and cook for about five minutes. Remove from heat and cool.

To freeze: Put the fish and the sauce in an airtight plastic container. Seal, label and freeze.

To serve: Thaw the fish overnight in the refrigerator or for four hours at room temperature. Pour the sauce into a saucepan and stir in the milk. Add the fish and cook over a low heat until the fish is warmed through.

Serves 4-6.

Shrimp with Tomatoes and Mushrooms

2 lb (1 kg) peeled shrimp
4 tablespoons oil
1 lb (500 g) tomatoes, chopped
2½ tablespoons chopped parsley
1 lb (500 g) mushrooms, sliced

1 teaspoon salt
½ teaspoon pepper
4 teaspoons plain flour
1 cup (250 ml) white wine
2 cloves garlic, minced

1. De-vein the shrimp and rinse quickly under running water. Drain and pat dry.
2. Cook shrimp in hot oil for five minutes. Remove from pan and keep warm.
3. Saute the tomatoes, chopped parsley, mushrooms, salt and pepper for about five minutes.
4. Mix the flour with a little of the wine. Then add the rest of the wine and add to the vegetables, stirring constantly. Cook until thickened.
5. Add the shrimp, cover and simmer for ten minutes. Cool.

To freeze: Put in an airtight plastic container. Seal, label and freeze.

To serve: Thaw overnight in the refrigerator or six hours at room temperature. Add the garlic and heat in a covered saucepan for 15 minutes.

Serves 6-8.

Curried Snapper

2 medium onions, chopped
3 tablespoons (45 g) butter
1 lb (500 g) snapper fillets
4 teaspoons curry powder

4 teaspoons plain flour
1½ cups (375 ml) fish stock
4 tablespoons lemon juice
1 cooking apple, sliced

1. Saute the onions in the butter until the onions are transparent.
2. Add the snapper fillets and cook for about four minutes on each side. Remove the fish from the pan.
3. Sprinkle on the curry powder and the flour and mix well.
4. Slowly add the fish stock, stirring constantly. Cook until thickened.
5. Return the fish to the pan and add the lemon juice and the sliced apple. Cover and simmer for five minutes. Cool.

To freeze: Put in an airtight container. Seal, label and freeze.

To serve: Thaw overnight in the refrigerator or thaw for five hours at room temperature. Put in a heavy-bottomed saucepan or the top of a double boiler over simmering water and heat through.

Serves 4.

Salmon and Rice

1 cup rice
1 lb (500 g) canned salmon
½ cup (125 g) butter, melted
1 teaspoon grated lemon rind

salt and pepper
3 hard-boiled egg yolks
2½ tablespoons chopped
  parsley

1. Cook the rice in boiling salted water until tender. Drain.
2. Break up the salmon and combine with the rice, butter, lemon rind, salt and pepper to taste, the mashed egg yolks and parsley.

To freeze: Put into a plastic container and cover. Seal, label and freeze.

To serve: Thaw for about three hours in the refrigerator. Put in the top of a double boiler and heat over simmering water.

Serves 4.

Fish Pie

1 lb (500 g) frozen puff pastry
1¼ cups (300 ml) white sauce
4 teaspoons capers,
  chopped
2½ tablespoons chopped
  parsley

4 teaspoons lemon juice
1 cup grated cheese
1 teaspoon pepper
1 lb (500 g) smoked fish

1. Thaw the pastry and roll out ¾ of it and line a pie dish.
2. Combine the white sauce, capers, parsley, lemon juice, cheese and pepper in a saucepan. Heat through.
3. Flake the fish and add to the sauce. Cook over a low heat for about seven minutes.
4. Pour into the pie shell.
5. Roll out the remaining pastry and put on top. Prick with a fork to allow steam to escape.
6. Cook in a 350°F (190°C) oven for about ½ hour. Cool.

To freeze: Remove from the tin, wrap in aluminum foil and seal. Label and freeze.

To serve: Butter the same pie dish and heat the pie in the dish for about ½ hour in a 350°F (180°C) oven.

Serves 4.

Fish with Almonds

2 lb (1 kg) fish fillets	3 teaspoons soy sauce
4 tablespoons (60 g) butter	¼ lb (125 g) bean sprouts
1 cup (250 ml) white wine	¼ lb (125 g) almonds,
4 teaspoons cornstarch	blanched
1 teaspoon almond essence	salt and pepper
2½ tablespoons chopped	
parsley	

1. Saute the fish in the butter for four minutes on each side. Remove from the pan.
2. Mix together the white wine, cornstarch, almond essence, parsley and soy sauce in the pan. Bring to a boil. Reduce heat and, stirring constantly, cook until thick.
3. Add the bean sprouts, almonds, salt and pepper and cook for five minutes.
4. Add the fish, cover and cook over a low heat for ten minutes. Cool.

To freeze: Place in an airtight container. Seal, label and freeze.

To serve: Thaw overnight in the refrigerator or for six hours at room temperature. Put into a heavy-bottomed saucepan or into the top of a double boiler over simmering water and heat through.

Serves 6-8.

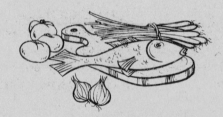

French Sole

4 leeks, chopped	1 teaspoon pepper
4 tablespoons (60 g) butter	1 bay leaf
1 lb (500 g) sole fillets	1 teaspoon salt
4 teaspoons plain flour	1 cup (250 ml) white sauce
1 cup (250 ml) white wine	½ cup grated cheese
1 teaspoon aniseed	chopped chives
½ teaspoon sage	

CONTINUED ON OPPOSITE PAGE

1. Saute the leeks in the butter for five minutes.
2. Add the fish and cook for three minutes on each side. Remove from the pan.
3. Mix the flour with a little of the wine, then mix in the rest of the wine and pour into the pan. Stir until thickened.
4. Stir in the aniseed, sage, pepper, bay leaf and salt. Cook over a medium heat for five minutes. Cool.

To freeze: Place in an airtight container. Seal, label and freeze.

To serve: Thaw overnight in the refrigerator or for six hours at room temperature. Mix together the white sauce and the grated cheese. Add to the fish and sauce. Cover and gently heat in a saucepan. Garnish with chopped chives.

Serves 4.

Fish in White Wine

4 leeks, chopped	1 teaspoon thyme
4 tablespoons (60 g) butter	1 teaspoon rosemary
1 lb (500 g) fish fillets	1½ teaspoons salt
3 medium carrots, chopped	1 teaspoon pepper
1 cup (250 ml) white wine	2 cloves garlic, minced
2 bay leaves	

1. Saute the leeks in the butter for five minutes.
2. Add the fish and cook for three minutes on each side. Remove the fish and leeks from the pan.
3. Put the carrots in the pan and cook for five minutes.
4. Add the wine, bay leaves, thyme, rosemary, salt and pepper. Cook for another five minutes.
5. Add the fish and leeks and cook over a low heat for a further five minutes. Cool.

To freeze: Place in an airtight container. Seal, label and freeze.

To serve: Thaw overnight in the refrigerator or for six hours at room temperature. Place in a saucepan, gently stir in the garlic and heat through.

Serves 4.

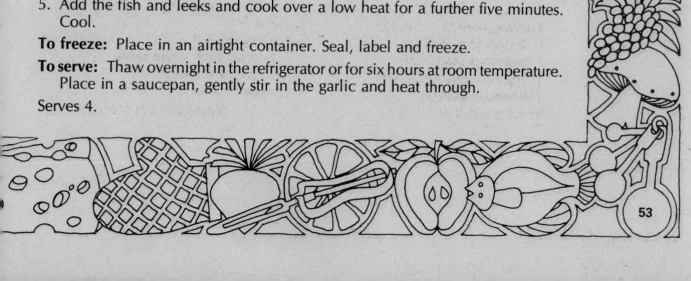

Salmon Patties

1 lb (500 g) canned salmon
2 cups mashed potatoes
2 small onions, minced
2½ tablespoons chopped
  parsley
3 teaspoons lemon juice

½ teaspoon salt
¼ teaspoon pepper
plain flour
1 egg, beaten
bread crumbs

1. Break up the salmon in a large bowl.
2. Add the potatoes, onions, parsley, lemon juice, salt and pepper.
3. Form into patties.
4. Coat the patties with the flour, dip into the beaten egg and then roll in bread crumbs.

To freeze: Wrap the patties in a single layer in aluminum foil (or in layers with plastic between the layers). Seal, label and freeze.

To serve: Shallow fry the frozen patties in hot oil until golden brown.

Serves 4.

Salmon Quiche

½ lb (250 g) shortcrust pastry
½ lb (250 g) canned salmon
2½ tablespoons chopped
  parsley
1 teaspoon pepper
½ lb (250 g) bacon

1 cup (250 ml) cream
4 eggs, beaten
1½ teaspoons salt
1 cup (125 g) grated cheddar
  cheese

1. Roll out the pastry and line a pie tin. Trim the edges.
2. Mix together the salmon, parsley and pepper.
3. Chop the bacon and fry for five minutes over a medium heat.
4. Add the salmon mixture to the bacon and mix well. Cook over a medium heat, stirring often, for ten minutes.
5. Put the mixture in the pastry shell and cook in a 350°F (180°C) oven for 15 minutes. Cool.

To freeze: Wrap securely in aluminum foil, seal, label and freeze.

To serve: Thaw at room temperature for 2-3 hours. Mix together the cream, eggs, and salt. Sprinkle the cheese on top of the salmon mixture, then pour on the cream and eggs. Bake in a 350°F (180°C) oven for ½ hour or until the quiche is set.

Serves 4.

Vegetables

Guide for Freezing Vegetables

It is necessary to blanch vegetables before freezing. You will need a large saucepan and a wire mesh basket which fits the saucepan. Vegetables are submerged in lightly salted boiling water. The water is then returned to a boil and the vegetables are cooked for the required length of time. The vegetables must then be put into ice water and left for the same length of time as they were blanched. Drain well and pat dry. The vegetables should then be put into a plastic bag and tied tightly with a wire tie.

Preparation of Vegetables for Freezing

Artichokes: For whole artichokes, remove coarse outer leaves and cut off the thorny tips. Trim the stems. Blanch for ten minutes in boiling water with ½ cup lemon juice added. Chill and pack in plastic bags.

Asparagus: Snap off the tough ends of the stalk. Wash several times and blanch for from 2-4 minutes depending on the size of the asparagus. Chill and pack in plastic bags.

Beans, green: Wash and cut off ends. Either cut into 1-inch (2½-cm) pieces or leave whole. Blanch for 2-3 minutes. Chill and pack in plastic bags.

Beans, Lima: Shell and wash beans. Blanch for 2-4 minutes. Chill and pack in plastic bags.

Beets: Cut off tops. Peel. If small, leave whole or slice or dice. Blanch for 3-5 minutes depending on size. Chill and pack in plastic bags.

Broccoli: Trim outer leaves and wash thoroughly. Cut the large stalks to a thickness of ½ inch (5 mm). Blanch for 3-4 minutes. Chill and pack in plastic bags.

Brussels Sprouts: Remove outer leaves and wash well. Blanch for 3-5 minutes depending on size. Chill and pack in plastic bags.

Cabbage: Remove outer leaves and cut into quarters or convenient-sized pieces. Blanch for 3-4 minutes depending on size. Chill and pack in plastic bags.

Carrots: Remove tops. Peel unless very young and tender. Leave small carrots whole; slice or dice larger carrots. If whole, blanch for five minutes. If sliced or diced, blanch for three minutes. Chill and pack in plastic bags.

Cauliflower: Remove outer leaves and cut into flowerets. Soak in cold water for five minutes then blanch for three minutes in boiling water to which two tablespoons of lemon juice or white vinegar has been added. Chill and pack in plastic bags.

Celery (good only for use later in cooking:) Remove coarse string and wash well. Cut into 2-inch (5-cm) lengths. Blanch for 3-4 minutes. Chill and pack in plastic bags.

Corn: For corn on the cob: remove husk and silk and trim ends. Blanch for 5-8 minutes depending on size. Chill and freeze separately, then pack in plastic bags. For corn kernels: Remove husk and silk and blanch whole ears for four minutes. Cool quickly and cut kernels from the cob. Pack in plastic bags.

Eggplant: Peel and cut into slices or cubes. Blanch for 2-4 minutes depending on size. Cool. Dip into a mixture of ¼ cup (65 ml) lemon juice and 2½ cups (625 ml) water to prevent discolouring. Drain and pat dry. Chill and pack in plastic bags. If you have sliced the eggplant, put a piece of plastic wrap between each slice before freezing.

Kohlrabi: Use small firm roots 2-3 inches (5-8 cm) in diameter. Cut off tops, peel and dice. Blanch for 1½ minutes. Chill and pack in plastic bags.

Leeks (good only for use later in cooking): Trim ends and remove outer leaves. Cut into ½-inch (1-cm) slices and wash well. Blanch for 2-4 minutes depending on size or saute in butter or oil. Chill and pack in plastic bags.

Mushrooms: Button mushrooms: Wipe clean. Leave whole. It is not necessary to blanch small mushrooms. If you do, blanch for two minutes. Chill and pack in plastic bags.
Large mushrooms: Wipe clean and slice. Blanch for 2-4 minutes in boiling water to which 1-2 tablespoons of lemon juice has been added. Or saute in butter or margarine. Chill and pack in plastic bags.

Onions (good only for use later in cooking): Peel and chop. Do not blanch. Pack in plastic bags.

Parsnips: Cut off tops and peel. Cut into slices, strips or cubes. Blanch for two minutes but chill for five minutes. Drain and pack in plastic bags.

Peas: Use only young sweet peas. Shell and blanch for 1½ minutes. Chill and pack in plastic bags.

Peppers (red and green): Remove stems and seeds. Cut in halves or slices. Do not blanch. Pack in plastic bags.

Potatoes: Fried: Peel and cut into strips. Fry in deep oil for two minutes. Drain well, cool and pack in plastic bags.

Spinach: Wash several times under cold running water. Cut off heavy stems. Blanch for 1½ minutes. Chill and drain well. Pack in plastic bags.

Tomatoes: Purée: Peel and simmer in their own juices for five minutes. Sieve or puree in an electric blender. Cool and pack in plastic containers.
Juice: Trim, quarter and simmer for ten minutes. Press through a nylon sieve and season with salt (1 teaspoon for every 1 quart of juice). Cool and pack in plastic containers.

Turnips: Trim and peel. Cut into 1 inch (2½-cm) cubes and blanch for 3 minutes. Chill and pack in plastic bags.

Zucchini: Cut into ½-inch (1-cm) slices. Blanch for 1½ minutes or saute in butter. Chill and drain well. Pack in plastic bags.

Tomatoes and Cauliflower

1 medium onion, chopped	salt and pepper
2½ tablespoons oil	10 black olives, pitted
1 lb (500 g) tomatoes	½ cauliflower
⅔ cup (165 ml) chicken stock	

1. Saute the onion in the oil until golden brown.
2. Add the tomatoes and cook over a low heat for five minutes.
3. Add the chicken stock, salt and pepper to taste and the olives. Mix well and simmer for about ten minutes.
4. Cut the cauliflower into flowerets and cook in boiling salted water for five minutes. Drain and put into a plastic container.
5. Pour the tomatoes over the cauliflower and cool.

To freeze: Seal the container, label and freeze.

To serve: Thaw for several hours at room temperature and heat gently in a saucepan. Or put into a casserole dish frozen and heat in a 325°F (160°C) oven until well heated.

Serves 4-6.

Ratatouille

3 onions, chopped	2 small eggplants, sliced
⅓ cup (85 ml) oil	6 zucchinis, sliced
3 green peppers, sliced	salt and pepper
1 lb (500 g) tomatoes, quartered	1 clove garlic, minced

1. Saute the onions in the oil until golden brown.
2. Add the green peppers, tomatoes, eggplants, zucchini and salt and pepper to taste.
3. Cover and cook over a low heat until the vegetables are just cooked.
4. Cool and skim off any oil.

To freeze: Put into a plastic container. Cover, seal, label and freeze.

To serve: Thaw at room temperature for several hours. When thawed, stir in the minced garlic. Put in a saucepan and simmer for five minutes.

Serves 6-8.

Louisiana Green Beans

2 lb (1 kg) fresh green beans	1 teaspoon lemon juice
4 tablespoons (60 g) butter	1 teaspoon Tabasco sauce
2 small onions, sliced	salt and pepper
1 green pepper, sliced	½ teaspoon brown sugar
½ lb (250 g) tomatoes, sliced	

1. Cook the prepared beans (uncut) in boiling salted water until just tender. Drain and put into a plastic container.
2. Melt the butter in a frypan and saute the onions until transparent.
3. Add the green pepper and cook for three minutes.
4. Add the remaining ingredients and mix well. Cook for five minutes. Pour over the beans and cool.

To freeze: Seal the plastic container, label and freeze.

To serve: Either defrost first and heat in a saucepan on top of the stove or put the frozen vegetables in the top of a double boiler and heat over simmering water.

Serves 6.

Stuffed Potatoes

4 large potatoes	1 egg, beaten
¼ lb (125 g) bacon, chopped	½ cup grated cheese
1 medium onion, minced	salt and pepper
1 teaspoon prepared mustard	paprika

1. Bake the potatoes in a 400°F (200°C) oven for about 1½ hours or until soft. Cut in half and scoop out the flesh taking care not to break the skin.
2. Fry the bacon for five minutes.
3. Add the onion and cook for another five minutes.
4. Mash the potatoes and add the bacon, onion, mustard, egg, cheese and salt and pepper to taste. Mix well.
5. Fill the potato skins with this mixture and sprinkle with paprika.

To freeze: Wrap the potatoes in aluminum foil. Seal, label and freeze.

To serve: Place the frozen potatoes wrapped in the foil in a 350°F (180°C) oven for 45 minutes. Remove the foil and bake for another 15 minutes or until the tops are browned.

Serves 4-8.

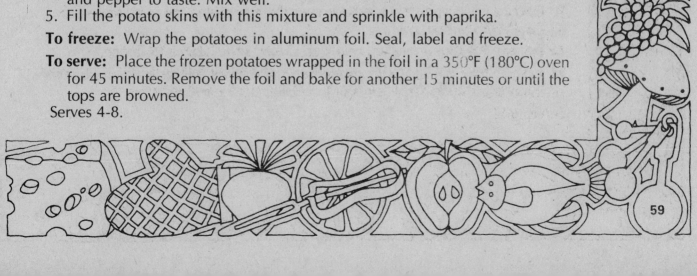

Potato Souffle

2 lb (1 kg) potatoes
4 tablespoons (60 g) butter
½ cup plain flour
salt and pepper
4 eggs, separated

1. Peel and cut the potatoes into chunks. Cook in boiling salted water until soft. Drain.
2. Mash the potatoes with the butter.
3. Add the flour and season to taste with salt and pepper. Mix well.
4. Slightly beat the egg yolks and add to the potato mixture.
5. Beat the egg whites until stiff and gently fold into the potato mixture.
6. Butter a 1½ quart souffle dish and pour the mixture into it.

To freeze: Cover the dish with aluminum foil, seal well, label and freeze.

To serve: Allow the souffle to thaw for about 1½ hours at room temperature. Remove the aluminum foil and bake in a 350°F (180°C) oven for ½ hour. Then raise the heat to 400°F (200°C) and cook for another ½ hour or until the souffle has risen and is golden brown.

Serves 6.

Corn Fritters

1 cup plain flour
¼ teaspoon salt
2 eggs, lightly beaten
milk

1 can (approx. 250 g) corn
   niblets or
6 oz (185 g) frozen corn, thawed
oil for frying

1. Sift together the flour and the salt into a bowl.
2. Add the eggs and enough milk to make a stiff batter.
3. Add the corn and mix well.
4. Heat a little oil in a frypan. Drop the corn fritter mixture by the spoonful into the frypan and fry until golden brown. Drain and cool.

To freeze: Arrange the fritters in layers in a plastic container with plastic wrap or freezer paper between the layers. Seal, label and freeze.

To serve: Place the frozen fritters on a baking tray and heat in a 350°F (180°C) oven for about 20 minutes.

Serves 4.

Creamed Peas with Mushrooms

1 lb (500 g) frozen peas
½ lb (250 g) bacon, chopped
¼ lb (125 g) mushrooms,
   chopped

salt and pepper
1½ tablespoons chopped
   parsley
⅔ cup (165 ml) cream

1. Cook the peas in boiling salted water for three minutes. Drain.
2. Cook the bacon in a frypan for five minutes.
3. Add the mushrooms and cook over a medium heat for 7 minutes.
4. Add the bacon and mushrooms to the peas.
5. Season to taste with salt and pepper and add the parsley. Cool.
6. When cool, stir in the cream.

To freeze: Put into a plastic container. Cover, seal, label and freeze.

To serve: Thaw for several hours at room temperature and gently heat in a saucepan or put frozen peas in the top of a double boiler and heat over simmering water.

Serves 4.

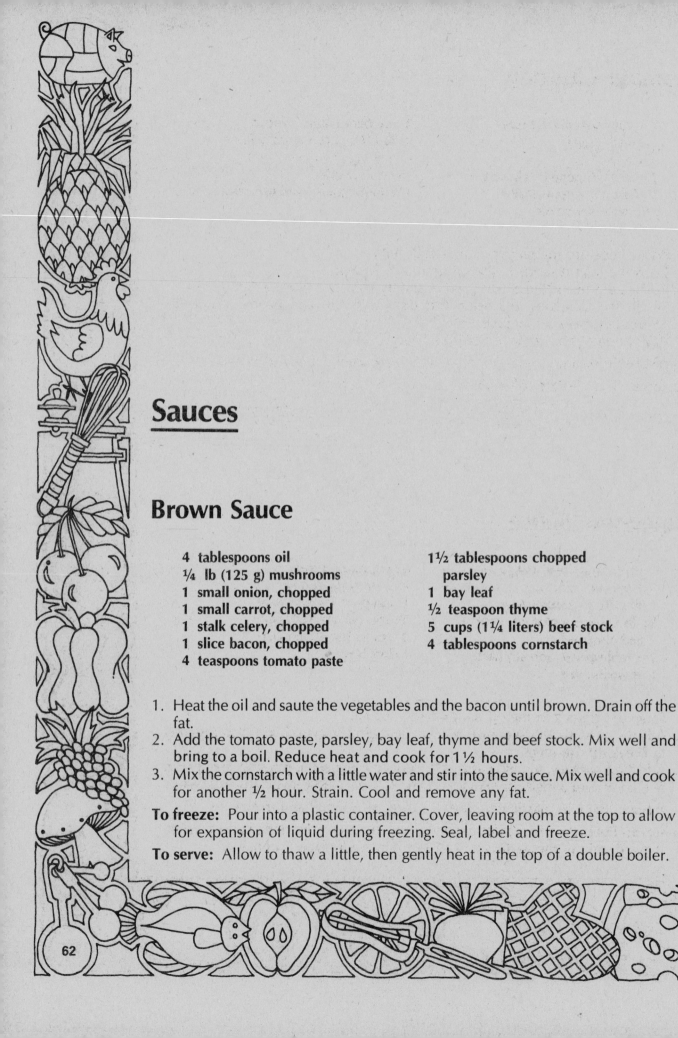

Sauces

Brown Sauce

4 tablespoons oil
¼ lb (125 g) mushrooms
1 small onion, chopped
1 small carrot, chopped
1 stalk celery, chopped
1 slice bacon, chopped
4 teaspoons tomato paste

1½ tablespoons chopped
  parsley
1 bay leaf
½ teaspoon thyme
5 cups (1¼ liters) beef stock
4 tablespoons cornstarch

1. Heat the oil and saute the vegetables and the bacon until brown. Drain off the fat.
2. Add the tomato paste, parsley, bay leaf, thyme and beef stock. Mix well and bring to a boil. Reduce heat and cook for 1½ hours.
3. Mix the cornstarch with a little water and stir into the sauce. Mix well and cook for another ½ hour. Strain. Cool and remove any fat.

To freeze: Pour into a plastic container. Cover, leaving room at the top to allow for expansion of liquid during freezing. Seal, label and freeze.

To serve: Allow to thaw a little, then gently heat in the top of a double boiler.

Tomato Chutney

2 teaspoons minced fresh
 green ginger
4 cloves
1 red chilli pepper, chopped
1 teaspoon cumin seeds
2½ tablespoons oil

1 medium onion, minced
1 lb (500 g) tomatoes, peeled
 and chopped
salt and pepper
1½ tablespoons chopped mint

1. Pound together the ginger, cloves and chilli.
2. Cook the cumin seeds in the oil until they brown.
3. Add the onion and the crushed spices and fry until the onion is golden brown.
4. Stir in the tomatoes and season to taste with salt and pepper. Cook for 45 minutes over a low heat.
5. Add the mint and remove from the heat. Cool.

To freeze: Pour into a plastic container. Cover, seal, label and freeze.

To serve: Thaw in the refrigerator for about six hours.

Bolognese Sauce

2 medium onions, chopped
4 teaspoons oil
1 lb (500 g) ground beef
½ lb (250 g) tomatoes, peeled
 and chopped
2½ tablespoons tomato paste
1 teaspoon salt

½ teaspoon pepper
½ teaspoon oregano
1 teaspoon brown sugar
¼ cup (65 ml) red wine
2 cloves garlic, minced
1 bay leaf

1. Saute the onions in the oil until golden brown.
2. Add the meat and cook over a medium heat until browned, stirring constantly to break up the meat.
3. Add the tomatoes, tomato paste, salt, pepper, oregano, sugar and wine. Cover and cook over a medium heat for one hour. Cool and skim off any excess fat.

To freeze: Pack in plastic containers. Cover, seal, label and freeze.

To serve: Put in the top of a double boiler and thaw over simmering water. When thawed, mix in the garlic and bay leaf. Cook for about ½ hour.

Apple Sauce

3 cooking apples
2½ tablespoons lemon juice
2 tablespoons water
4 teaspoons butter
2½ tablespoons sugar
½ teaspoon cinnamon

1. Peel and core the apples. Cut into slices and put into a saucepan with the lemon juice, water, butter, sugar and cinnamon. Cook until tender.
2. Sieve through a nylon strainer or purée in an electric blender. Cool.

To freeze: Pour into a plastic container leaving ½ inch (one cm) of room at the top to allow for expansion during freezing. Cover, seal, label and freeze.

To serve: Thaw for three hours at room temperature.

Onion Sauce

2 teaspoons butter
1 medium onion, minced
4 teaspoons (20 g) butter
4 teaspoons cornstarch
1¼ cups (300 ml) milk
½ teaspoon salt

1. Saute the onion in the two teaspoons of butter until golden brown. Remove from heat and set aside.
2. Melt the 4 teaspoons of butter in a saucepan and stir in the cornstarch. Cook over a low heat for one minute. Remove from heat.
3. Stirring constantly, gradually add the milk to the cornstarch and butter mixture. Bring to a boil.
4. Add the onion, mix well and remove from the heat. Cool.

To freeze: Pour into a plastic container. Cover, seal, label and freeze.

To serve: Allow to thaw a little to facilitate removal from the container. Put into the top of a double boiler and gently heat, stirring frequently.

Peach Chutney

1½ cups sliced peaches	1 medium onion, chopped
3 cups (750 ml) water	½ teaspoon ginger
2 teaspoons salt	¼ teaspoon paprika
2½ tablespoons cider vinegar	5½ tablespoons lemon juice
1 cup sugar	⅓ cup (55 g) raisins

1. Let the peaches stand in the water and salt for one day. Drain.
2. Mix together the vinegar and sugar in a saucepan. Add the peaches and cook gently for ½ hour.
3. Remove the peaches from the liquid and add the onion, ginger, paprika, lemon juice and raisins. Cook until the mixture thickens slightly.
4. Return the peaches to the saucepan and mix thoroughly. **Bring to a boil**, then remove from heat and cool.

To freeze: Pour into a plastic container. Cover, seal, label and freeze.

To serve: Thaw overnight in the refrigerator.

Chocolate Sauce

½ lb (250 g) dark chocolate
1 cup sugar
3 tablespoons (45 g) butter
1 large can evaporated milk
1 egg, beaten

1. Melt the chocolate in the top of a double boiler over simmering water.
2. Mix in the sugar, butter and evaporated milk. Cook for three minutes.
3. Beat in the egg. Remove from heat and cool.

To freeze: Pour into a plastic container leaving ½ inch (one cm) of space at the top to allow for expansion of liquid during freezing. Cover, seal, label and freeze.

To serve: Allow to thaw a little to make it easier to remove from the container. Put into the top of a double boiler and heat gently, stirring constantly.

Brandy Sauce

2　cups (500 ml) water
⅔ cup brown sugar
1　lb (500 g) marmalade
grated rind of two lemons
½ cup (125 ml) lemon juice
½ cup (125 ml) brandy

1. Mix together the water, sugar, marmalade and lemon rind in a saucepan. Bring to a boil. Reduce the heat and simmer for 15 minutes.
2. Strain the sauce.
3. Stir in the lemon juice and brandy. Cool.

To freeze: Pour into a plastic container leaving one inch (2½ cm) of space at the top to allow to expansion of liquid during freezing. Cover, seal, label and freeze. Or pour the sauce into ice cube trays and freeze. When frozen, remove from tray and put into a plastic bag. Seal, label and return to the freezer.

To serve: If frozen in a plastic container, allow to thaw a little to make it easier to remove from the container. Gently heat in a saucepan. If frozen in cubes, remove the number required and heat gently.

Bechamel Sauce

2　cups (500 ml) milk
2　medium onions, quartered
10 peppercorns
1　medium carrot, chopped
3　tablespoons (45 g) butter
4　tablespoons plain flour
salt and pepper

1. Mix together the milk, onions, peppercorns and the carrot in a saucepan. Bring to a boil then remove from heat and allow to stand for 15 minutes. Strain.
2. Melt the butter in a saucepan and stir in the flour. Remove from heat and add the milk, stirring constantly.
3. Return to the heat and cook until the sauce has thickened.
4. Season to taste with salt and pepper.

To freeze: Pour the sauce into a plastic container. Cover and cool. Seal, label and freeze.

To serve: Allow to thaw a little, then put into a saucepan and gently heat.

Cheese Sauce

½ cup (125 g) butter
8 tablespoons plain flour
4 cups (1 liter) milk
2 cups grated cheese
salt and pepper

1. Melt the butter in a large saucepan and stir in the flour. Cook over a low heat for one minute.
2. Remove the pan from the heat and, stirring constantly, gradually add the milk. Beat until smooth.
3. Return to the heat and add the cheese. Stir until the cheese has melted and the sauce is thick.
4. Season to taste with salt and pepper.

To freeze: Pour the sauce into a plastic container. Put a piece of buttered waxed paper over the surface to prevent a skin from forming. Cool. Cover, seal, label and freeze.

To serve: Thaw in the container for a little while to make it easier to remove. Then put in the top of a double boiler over simmering water and heat thoroughly, stirring constantly to prevent the sauce from separating.

Madeira Sauce

4 scallions, chopped
3 tablespoons (45 g) butter
4 tablespoons plain flour
2 cups (500 ml) beef stock
4 tablespoons tomato paste
salt and pepper
½ cup (125 ml) Madeira wine

1. Saute the scallions in the butter for two minutes.
2. Sprinkle on the flour, mix well and cook over a low heat for one minute.
3. Add the stock, the tomato paste and salt and pepper to taste. Simmer for three minutes.
4. Stir in the Maderia. Cool.

To freeze: Pour into a plastic container leaving about one inch (2½ cm) of space at the top to allow for expansion of the liquid during the freezing. Cover, seal, label and freeze.

To serve: Allow to thaw out a little, then turn into a saucepan and gently heat.

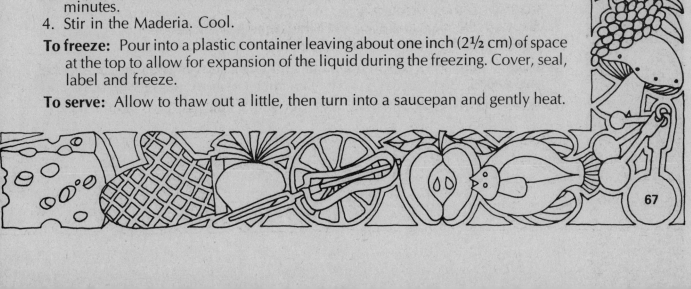

Cherry Sauce

    1 lb (500 g) dark cherries
    1 cup (250 ml) water
    ¾ cup sugar
    2 tablespoons cornstarch
    ½ teaspoon cinnamon

1. Wash the cherries well and remove the stones.
2. Put the cherries and the water in a saucepan and cook until the cherries are soft.
3. Sieve the cherries with the water through a nylon strainer or purée with the water in an electric blender. Pour back into the saucepan.
4. Stir in the sugar.
5. Mix the cornstarch and cinnamon with a little water and mix into the cherries.
6. Boil for five minutes or until the sauce has thickened.

To freeze: Pour the sauce into a plastic container, cover and cool. Leave ½ inch (one cm) of space at the top to allow for the expansion of the liquid during freezing. Seal, label and freeze. Or pour the sauce into ice cube trays and, when cool, put into the freezer. When the cubes are frozen, remove from trays and put into a plastic bag. Seal, label and return to the freezer.

To serve: If frozen in a plastic container, allow to thaw a little before putting into a saucepan. Heat gently. If frozen into cubes, remove number required and heat in a saucepan.

Guide for Freezing Fruits

There are four ways to prepare fruit for freezing. The method used depends on the type of fruit and the subsequent use intended. Some fruits with thick skins such as gooseberries and currants may be simply washed, dried and packed in plastic bags, especially if they are to be used in cooking or for making jams. Adding sugar or sugar syrup will, however, help to keep the color and flavor of the fruit. It will also protect the fruit from oxidizing and thus lengthen its storage life.

The four methods are:

Freezing separately: This method is suitable for small whole fruits such as strawberries and raspberries. If the fruit must be washed, be sure it is thoroughly dried. Arrange the fruit in a single layer in a plastic bag on a baking tray. Put into the freezer and when frozen, shake down into the bag and fill with more fruit frozen in the same way. Seal tightly when the bag is full. Any quantity of fruit may be removed for use and the bag resealed.

Freezing in dry sugar: Clean and dry the fruit. Sprinkle with sugar. Usually the ratio of sugar to fruit is ¼ lb (125 g) sugar to 1 lb (500 g) fruit but this can be varied depending on your taste and the sweetness of the fruit. Make sure the fruit is evenly coated with the sugar, then pack into plastic bags or waxed cartons and seal.

Freezing in sugar syrup: The sugar syrup should be made and cooled completely before being added to the fruit. You should allow at least 1 cup (250 ml) of syrup to each 1 lb (500 g) of fruit.

Light syrup — 1 cup (250 g) sugar to 2½ cups (625 ml) water
Medium sugar syrup — 1½ cups (375 g) sugar to 2½ cups water
Heavy sugar syrup — 2¼ cups (565 g) sugar to 2½ cups water

To make the syrup, mix together the sugar and water in a saucepan and bring to a boil. Simmer, stirring constantly, only until sugar is dissolved. Cover the saucepan and allow to cool completely before adding to the fruit. If necessary, add the ascorbic acid solution at this point.

Put the fruit in plastic or waxed containers and pour the syrup over the fruit. Stir to make sure that all the fruit is coated. If the fruit is floating in the syrup, crumple some waxed paper and put on top of the fruit before putting on the lid. This will keep the fruit submerged. Do not fill the container right up to the top with syrup. Leave about 1 inch (2½-cm) of space between the syrup and the lid of the container to allow for the expansion of the liquid during freezing.

Purées and Juices: This method is good for over-ripe fruit or fruit that has been bruised. Fruit is pressed through a nylon sieve. (Apples should be cooked first.) Sugar can be added according to taste: ½ cup (125 g) sugar for each 1 lb (500 g) of fruit. Pour the purée or juice into a plastic container, leaving room at the top to allow for expansion of the liquid during freezing, and seal.

To prevent discoloring of fruits, the fruit can be dipped into a solution of ascorbic acid and water (500 mg of ascorbic acid to 2½ cups of water). After dipping, drain, dry and freeze separately or in dry sugar. If fruit is to be packed in sugar syrup,

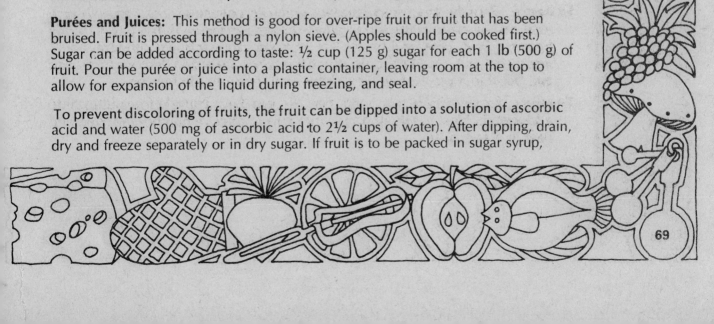

dissolve 500 mg of ascorbic in one tablespoon of cold water and stir into 2½ cups (625 ml) of cold sugar syrup.

Apples: Peel, core and slice. Dip in ascorbic acid solution to prevent discoloring. Blanch for 2-3 minutes. Chill. You may then freeze separately in dry sugar or in a medium sugar syrup. Pack into appropriate containers. Cover, seal, label and freeze.

Apricots: Peel the apricots and remove the stones. (To facilitate peeling, dip the apricots first in boiling water then into cold water. The skin should then pull off easily.) Pack in a plastic container in a medium sugar syrup with ascorbic acid solution added. Cover, seal, label and freeze.

Avocados: Peel and remove stone. Mash or puree in an electric blender. Add 2 teaspoons of lemon juice to each 2 cups of purée. Pack into containers. Cover, seal, label and freeze.

Blackberries: Remove the stalks. Wash and dry well. Freeze separately, freeze in dry sugar or freeze in heavy syrup. Pack appropriately. Seal, label and freeze.

Cherries: Wash and dry well. Remove stems and stones. Pack in light sugar syrup. Seal, label and freeze.

Currants: Wash and dry well. Remove stems. Freeze separately for jams and juice. Or freeze in dry sugar or heavy sugar syrup. Seal, label and freeze.

Coconuts: Break open husked coconut and remove meat. Grate or grind the meat. Put into plastic containers and press down. Cover, seal, label and freeze.

Dates: Remove pits. Wash and dry well. Pack in containers without syrup. Cover, seal, label and freeze.

Figs: Wash in very cold water. Remove stems and peel. To pack unsweetened, cover with ascorbic acid solution or first dip into ascorbic acid solution and then pack in dry sugar in containers. To pack sweetened, cover with medium sugar syrup with ascorbic acid solution added. Seal, label and freeze.

Gooseberries: Wash and dry fruit thoroughly. Pack separately for jam-making, pack in dry sugar for cooking or in heavy sugar syrup for desserts. Seal, label and freeze.

Grapes: Halve and remove the seeds. (Seedless varieties may be left whole.) Pack in light sugar syrup. Seal, label and freeze.

Grapefruit: Peel and remove all pith and seeds. Divide into segments. May be packed with dry sugar or light sugar syrup. Seal, label and freeze.

Lemons: Squeeze and pour the juice into ice cube trays. When frozen, put into plastic bags and remove as needed.

Mangoes: Peel and slice. Pack in light sugar syrup with lemon juice added. Seal, label and freeze. Serve with additional lemon juice.

Melons: Peel and remove seeds. Cut in slices, cubes or balls. Either sprinkle with lemon juice and pack in dry sugar or pack in light sugar syrup. Seal, label and freeze.

Nectarines: Peel, cut in halves and remove stones. Pack in medium sugar syrup with double strength ascorbic acid solution. If packing in dry sugar, dip in an ascorbic acid solution before sprinkling with dry sugar. Seal, label and freeze.

Oranges: Peel and remove pith. Divide into segments and remove seeds. Freeze separately. Or pack in medium sugar syrup. Or squeeze oranges and pour the juice into ice cube trays. When frozen put into a plastic bag and use as needed. Whole Seville oranges may be frozen to be used for marmalade. Seal, label and freeze.

Peaches: Peel, cut in halves or slices and remove stones. (Peeling is made easier by plunging the peaches first in boiling water, then in cold water. This does tend to discolor the flesh, though.) Peaches can be packed in a medium sugar syrup with double strength ascorbic acid added or they may be packed with dry sugar. Over-ripe peaches may be pureed in an electric blender or pressed through a nylon strainer. If pureed, add 4 teaspoons of lemon juice and ½ cup sugar for each 1 lb (500 g) of fruit used. Pack in suitable containers, seal, label and freeze.

Pears: Because pears become very soft after they are thawed, it is best to puree them only. Pack in containers, seal, label and freeze.

Pineapples: Peel and core. Remove eyes. Cut into slices, cubes or wedges. Pack in a light sugar syrup or crush pineapple and mix about ⅔ cup of sugar to each 1 lb (500 g) fruit. You may pack slices unsweetened but put a piece of freezer paper between each slice before packing in a plastic bag. Seal, label and freeze.

Plums: Wash and dry thoroughly. Halve and remove stones. Pack separately or with dry sugar for jam-making or for cooking. Pack in heavy sugar syrup with ascorbic acid solution added. Seal, label and freeze.

Rhubarb: Wash, trim and cut into desired lengths. Blanch for 2 minutes. Chill in ice water and drain well. Pack separately or with dry sugar for pies or preserves. Pack in heavy sugar syrup for desserts. Seal, label and freeze.

Strawberries: Choose firm strawberries. Remove stalks. Freeze separately or with dry sugar. You may puree the strawberries in an electric blender or press them through a nylon strainer. Add ½ cup sugar for each 1 lb (500 g) of fruit. Pour in a plastic container. Seal, label and freeze.

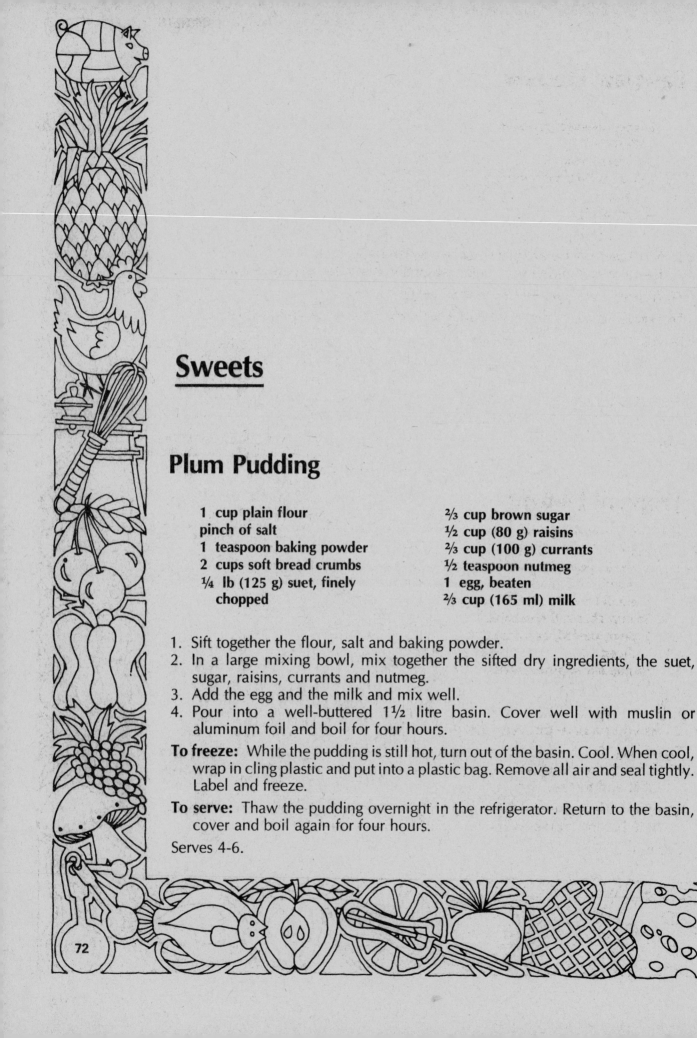

Sweets

Plum Pudding

1 cup plain flour
pinch of salt
1 teaspoon baking powder
2 cups soft bread crumbs
¼ lb (125 g) suet, finely chopped

⅔ cup brown sugar
½ cup (80 g) raisins
⅔ cup (100 g) currants
½ teaspoon nutmeg
1 egg, beaten
⅔ cup (165 ml) milk

1. Sift together the flour, salt and baking powder.
2. In a large mixing bowl, mix together the sifted dry ingredients, the suet, sugar, raisins, currants and nutmeg.
3. Add the egg and the milk and mix well.
4. Pour into a well-buttered 1½ litre basin. Cover well with muslin or aluminum foil and boil for four hours.

To freeze: While the pudding is still hot, turn out of the basin. Cool. When cool, wrap in cling plastic and put into a plastic bag. Remove all air and seal tightly. Label and freeze.

To serve: Thaw the pudding overnight in the refrigerator. Return to the basin, cover and boil again for four hours.

Serves 4-6.

Pawpaw Dessert

8 cups mashed pawpaw
   flesh
3½ cups sugar
1¼ cups (300 ml) lemon
   juice
4 egg whites

1. Mix together the pawpaw, sugar and lemon juice.
2. Beat the egg whites until stiff and gently fold into the pawpaw mixture.

To freeze: Pour into ice trays and freeze.

To serve: Allow to thaw only until soft enough to scoop out and serve.

Serves 8.

Tropical Delight

1½ cups (375 ml) rosé wine
1 apple, peeled, cored and
   diced
1 small banana, sliced
½ cup chopped pineapple
1 pear, peeled, cored and
   diced
½ cup sliced strawberries

1. Pour the wine into a large bowl.
2. As you prepare the fruit, add to the wine.

To freeze: Put the fruit and wine in a plastic container. Allow 1 inch (2½-cm) of space at the top to allow for expansion of liquid during freezing. Cover, seal, label and freeze.

To serve: Thaw in the refrigerator. Delicious served with whipped cream and a little brandy sprinkled on the top of each serving.

Serves 4.

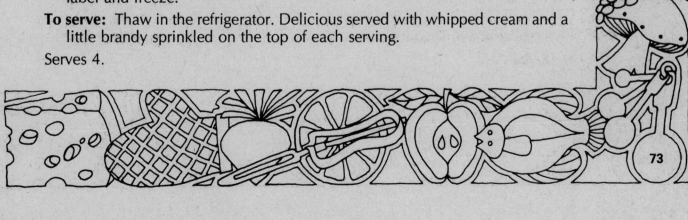

Peach Cheesecake

4 tablespoons (60 g) butter
2 cups cookie crumbs
¼ cup confectioners' sugar
2 teaspoons gelatin
¼ cup (65 ml) cold water
2 eggs, separated
½ teaspoon vanilla essence
4 tablespoons sugar

½ cup (125 ml) cream
1½ cups cottage cheese
1½ teaspoons grated lemon
   rind
4 tablespoons lemon juice
¼ cup sugar
1 can (470 g) sliced peaches

1. Mix the butter with 1½ cups of cookie crumbs and the confectioners' sugar. Press the mixture with the back of a spoon or with your fingertips on the bottom and sides of a springform pan. Place in the refrigerator.
2. Soak the gelatin in the cold water for five minutes.
3. Lightly beat the egg yolks and combine with the vanilla essence, sugar and half freezing cream in the top of a double boiler. Place over simmering water and cook, stirring constantly, until thickened. Remove from heat.
4. Stir the gelatin and water into the egg yolk mixture until dissolved.
5. Put the cottage cheese into a large mixing bowl and pour the mixture from the double boiler over it. Mix gently.
6. Lightly whip the rest of the cream and fold into the cheese mixture with the lemon rind and lemon juice.
7. Beat the egg whites until stiff, add the sugar and beat until the sugar is mixed in. Fold into cheese mixture.
8. Pour half the mixture into the prepared crust. Arrange drained peaches over it, then pour on remaining mixture. Sprinkle with the remaining ½ cup of biscuit crumbs.

To freeze: Place in a plastic container with a lid. Seal, label and freeze.

To serve: Thaw in container in refrigerator for about six hours. Serve chilled.

Serves 6-8.

Coffee Creams

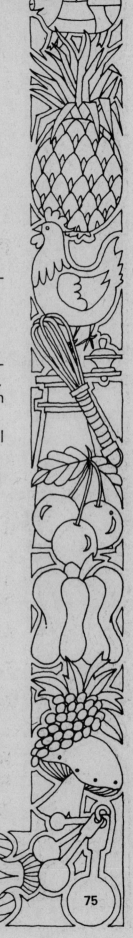

2 cups cake flour	4 teaspoons hot water
¼ teaspoon salt	3 tablespoons (45 g) butter
1 egg	½ cup confectioners' sugar
½ cup (125 g) butter	1 tablespoon cream
½ cup sugar	½ teaspoon instant coffee
1½ teaspoons instant coffee	2 teaspoons hot water

1. Sift together the flour and salt.
2. Beat the egg until light yellow.
3. Cream together the butter and sugar until light and fluffy.
4. Add the beaten egg to the butter and sugar.
5. Dissolve the instant coffee in the tablespoon of hot water and add to the mixture.
6. Add the flour and mix thoroughly.
7. Drop by the teaspoonful onto a greased baking tray.
8. Bake in a 325°F (160°C) oven for about 15 minutes. Cool.
9. Make butter cream by blending together the three tablespoons butter, confectioners' sugar, cream and the instant coffee dissolved in the hot water.
10. When the biscuits are cooled, make a sandwich of two biscuits spread with the butter cream.

To freeze: First freeze uncovered on a tray, then put in a plastic bag and seal tightly. Label and return to the freezer.

To serve: Thaw in plastic bag for ½ hour, then put on serving dish.

Iced Strawberry Mousse

½ lb (250 g) strawberries
2 tablespoons sugar
4 egg yolks
⅔ cup (165 ml) cream
2 teaspoons lemon juice
2 egg whites

1. Sieve the strawberries or purée in an electric blender.
2. Put in the top of a double boiler over hot water or in a bowl over hot water. Add the sugar and egg yolks and beat until thickened.
3. Remove from the heat and beat occasionally while the strawberry mixture is cooling.
4. Lightly whip the cream and fold into the strawberry mixture.
5. Gently add the lemon juice.
6. Beat the egg whites until stiff but not dry. Fold into the strawberry mixture.

To freeze: Pour into a plastic dish and cover tightly. Seal, label and freeze.

To serve: Remove from the freezer and thaw in the refrigerator ½ hour before serving. Serves 6.

Lemon Souffle

¾ tablespoons gelatin
4 tablespoons water
4 eggs, separated
½ cup sugar

⅔ cup (165 ml) lemon juice
grated rind of one lemon
1½ cups (375 ml) cream
chopped nuts to garnish

1. Mix the gelatin with the water and allow to soak.
2. Mix together the egg yolks, sugar and lemon juice in the top of a double boiler. Place over boiling water and cook, stirring constantly, until thickened.
3. Stir in the gelatin and mix until dissolved. Remove from the heat.
4. Add the lemon rind and cool.
5. Whip the cream and add to the lemon mixture.
6. Beat the egg whites until stiff and fold into the souffle.

To freeze: Pour into a souffle dish or a plastic container and put in the freezer uncovered until set. Sprinkle on the nuts, cover, seal, label and freeze.

To serve: Allow to thaw for three hours at room temperature. Serves 6-8.

Nut-Fruit Crumble

½ cup (125 g) butter
2 cups plain flour
½ cup brown sugar
pinch of salt

½ cup chopped nuts
2 lb (1 kg) fruit (apples,
   peaches, plums, etc.)
sugar to taste

1. Mix together the softened butter, flour, sugar, salt and nuts.
2. Peel and cut the fruit and cook in boiling water until just tender. Drain and add sugar to taste.
3. Put the fruit in an oven-proof dish. Put nut mixture on the top and press down.

To freeze: Cover, seal, label and freeze.

To serve: Allow to thaw for one hour at room temperature, uncovered. Bake in 325°F (160°C) oven for about 45 minutes or until heated through.

Pineapple Sponge Cake

2 large sponge cakes
2½ cups (625 ml) cream
1 lb (500 g) orange
   marmalade
1 can (825 g) pineapple
   pieces

1. Cut each sponge cake in half to make two layers.
2. Whip the cream and put in the refrigerator for about 3 hours. Pour off the water that has collected in the bottom of the bowl.
3. Spread the half of the sponges with cream and most of the marmalade. Drain the pineapple pieces and arrange on top of the marmalade. Place other half of sponge on top.
4. Press the remaining marmalade through a strainer and heat in a small saucepan. Brush this glaze on the top of the sponges.

To freeze: Put the cakes in plastic containers without a lid in the freezer for two hours. Then cover with the lid. Seal, label and freeze.

To serve: Thaw in the container with the lid on for about 3 hours. You may glaze the cakes again with the heated marmalade if you wish.

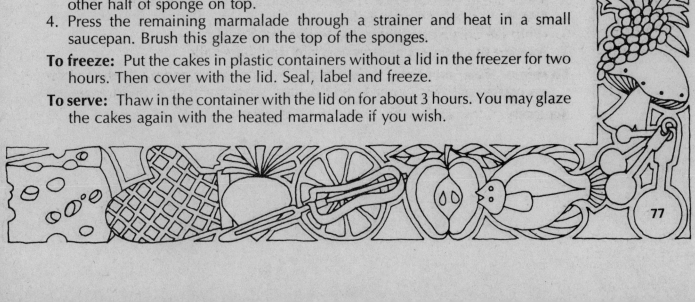

Apricot Flan

Pastry:
1½ cups plain flour
½ cup (125 g) butter
cold water

Filling:
½ lb (250 g) apricots
¼ cup sugar

4 tablespoons (60 g) butter
1 egg, beaten
½ teaspoon vanilla essence
½ cup cake flour
4 tablespoons apricot jam

1. Make the pastry by rubbing the butter into the flour until the mixture looks like fine bread crumbs. Add enough water to form a firm dough. Roll out and line an 7-inch (18-cm) flan tin. Reserve the scraps of pastry.
2. Remove the stones from the apricots and slice the fruit. Cook the apricots in a little water until soft. Strain and reserve the liquid. Cool the fruit.
3. Cream together the sugar and butter until light and fluffy.
4. Add the egg and vanilla essence.
5. Fold in the flour.
6. Arrange the apricots in the pastry shell and spread the sugar-butter-egg mixture over the top.
7. Roll out the scraps of pastry into long thin strips and put these in a lattice pattern on the top.
8. Bake in a 375°F (190°C) oven for about 50 minutes.
9. While the flan is cooking, heat together the apricot jam and two table-spoons of the reserved liquid from the apricots. When the flan is cooked, brush the top with a thick layer of this glaze. Cool.

To freeze: Wrap tightly in aluminum foil Seal, label and freeze.

To serve: Thaw overnight in the refrigerator or at room temperature for about six hours.

Serves 4.

Orange Sherbet

grated rind of one orange	1 teaspoon gelatin
1½ cups (375 ml) orange juice	4 teaspoons cold water
	¼ cup sugar
1½ cups (375 ml) cold water	2 egg whites

1. In a saucepan mix together the orange rind, orange juice and 1½ cups of cold water. Bring to a boil.
2. While the orange juice is heating, soak the gelatin in the four teaspoons of cold water.
3. Mix the gelatin and the sugar into the orange mixture. Stir until the gelatin is dissolved. Remove from heat and cool.
4. When the mixture is cool, put into freezer tray and place in freezer until almost hard.
5. Beat the egg whites until stiff and mix into the orange mixture.

To freeze: Return to the freezer trays, cover, label and freeze.

To serve: Remove from the freezer about half an hour before serving.

Serves 4-6.

Apple Strudel

3 medium cooking apples, peeled and chopped	⅓ cup brown sugar
2 tablespoons lemon juice	1 teaspoon mixed spice
⅓ cup (55 g) raisins	½ lb frozen puff pastry, thawed
⅓ cup (50 g) currants	3 tablespoons (45 g) butter

1. Mix together the apples, lemon juice, raisins, currants, sugar and mixed spice.
2. Roll out the pastry thinly in a square shape.
3. Spread the butter on the pastry.
4. Spread the apple filling on the pastry, leaving about ½ inch (1-cm) around the edges. Wet the edges and roll up.

To freeze: Wrap securely in aluminum foil. Label and freeze.

To serve: Remove the aluminum foil and place on a buttered baking tray. Cook in a 425°F (220°C) oven either frozen (for 45 minutes) or thawed (30 minutes).

Serves 4-6.

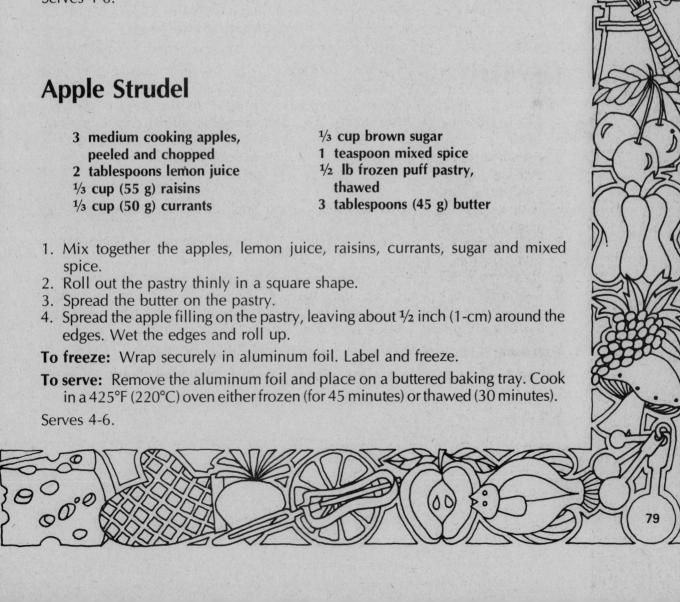

Caramel Custard

½ cup sugar
⅔ cup (165 ml) water
2½ cups (625 ml) milk
4 large eggs

1. Mix together the sugar and water in a small saucepan. Dissolve the sugar over a low heat, then bring to a boil and continue to boil until the mixture becomes golden brown.
2. Pour the caramelised sugar into a small freezer-to-oven dish, tipping the dish to cover the bottom evenly.
3. Warm the milk and pour in the eggs which have been lightly beaten.
4. Strain over the caramel in the dish. Cool.

To freeze: Cover the top with aluminum foil. Freeze. When frozen, wrap in a plastic bag. Seal and label.

To serve: Remove wrapping and put the custard in a tin of warm water. The water should come half-way up the sides of the dish. Bake in a 375°F (190°C) oven for about one hour or until set.

Jam Tart

6 oz (185 g) short-crust pastry
jam
4 tablespoons (60 g) butter
¼ cup sugar
1 egg

½ teaspoon vanilla essence
¼ teaspoon almond essence
⅔ cup cake crumbs
¼ cup (30 g) ground almonds

1. Butter an 7-inch (18-cm) cake tin.
2. Roll out the pastry and line the cake tin.
3. Spread a thick layer of jam on the pastry.
4. Mix together the butter and sugar. Beat until light and fluffy.
5. Beat in the egg, then add the vanilla essence, almond essence, cake crumbs and ground almonds. Mix well. Spoon this mixture on top of the jam.
6. Bake in a 350°F (180°C) oven for about 40 minutes. Cool.

To freeze: Turn out of the tin and wrap in aluminum foil. Seal, label and freeze.

To serve: Thaw at room temperature for about three hours.

Serves 6.

Almond Dessert

½ cup (125 g) butter
1 cup sugar
1 lb (500 g) cream cheese
5 eggs, separated
⅔ cup semolina
1 cup (110 g) ground
   almonds

grated rind of one lemon
4 tablespoons lemon juice
⅔ cup (120 g) raisins
¼ teaspoon almond essence

1. Cream together the butter and sugar until light and fluffy.
2. Add the softened cream cheese and beat well.
3. Beat the egg yolks and add to the cheese mixture.
4. Stir in the semolina, ground almonds, lemon rind, lemon juice, raisins and almond essence.
5. Beat the egg whites until stiff and gently fold into the mixture.
6. Pour the mixture into a 8-inch (20-cm) cake tin and bake in a 350°F (180°C) oven for about 45 minutes. Cool and turn out of the tin.

To freeze: Wrap in aluminum foil. Seal, label and freeze.

To serve: Thaw overnight in the refrigerator or at room temperature for about three hours.

Serves 6.

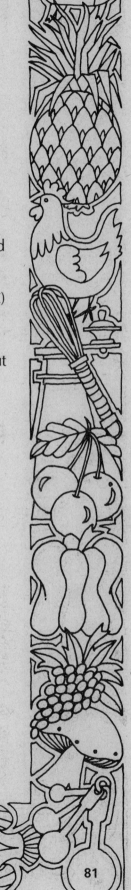

Raspberry Mousse

2 cans (470 g) raspberries,
   drained
4 teaspoons gelatin
⅔ cup (165 ml) hot water
sugar to taste
2 egg whites

1. Mash the raspberries or purée in an electric blender.
2. Soak the gelatin in the hot water until cool.
3. Combine the gelatin with the raspberries. Mix well.
4. Add sugar to taste. Put aside until almost set.
5. Beat the egg whites until stiff, then gently fold into the raspberry mixture.

To freeze: Pour into a plastic container. Cover, seal, label and freeze.

To serve: Thaw in the refrigerator overnight or for three hours at room temperature.

Serves 4.

Bread and Butter Pudding

8 slices white bread, crust   3 eggs
   removed   ¼ teaspoon cinnamon
butter   ¼ cup sugar
raisins   3 cups (750 ml) milk

1. Butter the bread and cut into strips.
2. Butter a 1½ quart oven-proof dish and place layers of the buttered bread and sultanas in it.
3. Beat together the eggs, cinnamon, sugar and milk.
4. Pour over the bread and allow to stand for 15 minutes.

To freeze: Cover, seal, label and freeze.

To serve: Thaw for 6 hours at room temperature. Bake in a 325°F (160°C) oven for about one hour or until set and golden brown.

Serves 4-6.

Almond Cookies

½ cup (125 g) butter
¾ cup sugar
1 egg
1 cup plain flour
1 teaspoon baking powder

1¼ teaspoons almond
   essence
⅔ cup (85 g) chopped
   almonds

1. Cream together the butter and sugar until light and fluffy.
2. Beat the egg and add to the butter and sugar mixture.
3. Stir in the flour, baking powder, almond essence and chopped almonds.
4. Shape mixture into small balls and place on a greased baking tray. Press the cookies down slightly.
5. Bake in a 400°F (200°C) for 8-10 minutes. Cool.

To freeze: Pack in a plastic bag, seal, label and freeze.

To serve: Remove from plastic and thaw at room temperature for about two hours.

Florentines

1½ tablespoons chopped glace
   cherries
4 tablespoons mixed peel
1 cup (125 g) chopped
   almonds

4 tablespoons (60 g) butter
¼ cup sugar
4 teaspoons honey
4 teaspoons cream
¼ lb (125 g) plain chocolate

1. Put all the ingredients except the chocolate together in a saucepan. Heat gently and stir until well mixed.
2. Butter a baking tray and spread the mixture evenly on the tray.
3. Bake in a 350°F (180°C) oven for about 8 minutes or until firm and golden brown.
4. Cut into desired size squares and, when slightly cooled, remove from tray and cool.
5. Melt the chocolate in a bowl over hot water. Coat the bottoms of the florentines with the chocolate and put upside-down to dry.

To freeze: When the chocolate is set, wrap in aluminum foil. Seal, label and freeze.

To serve: Remove from the foil and thaw at room temperature for about 45 minutes.

Cinnamon Nut Streusel

½ cup (125 g) butter
¾ cup caster sugar
1 egg, beaten
1⅔ cups cake flour
pinch of salt
⅔ cup (165 ml) milk
½ cup brown sugar

2 tablespoons melted butter
5½ tablespoons cake flour
1½ teaspoons cinnamon
⅔ cup (80 g) chopped walnuts

1. Butter and flour a cake tin 7 × 12 inches (18 × 30 cm).
2. Cream together the butter and sugar until light and fluffy.
3. Add the egg and mix well.
4. Sift together the flour and salt and add to the butter and sugar mixture with the milk. Beat well.
5. In a separate bowl combine the brown sugar, melted butter, flour, cinnamon and walnuts.
6. Pour half the cake mixture into the prepared tin. Sprinkle half the cinnamon-nut mixture on top. Pour on the remaining cake mixture and sprinkle with the remaining cinnamon-nut mixture.
7. Bake in a 350°F (180°C) oven for about 40 minutes. Cool.

To freeze: Remove the streusel from the tin and wrap in aluminum foil. Seal, label and freeze.

To serve: Remove the wrapping and allow to thaw at room temperature for about 3 hours.

Coffee Cookies

1 cup (250 g) butter
⅓ cup confectioners' sugar
4 teaspoons instant coffee
1½ cups plain flour
½ cup cornstarch

1. Cream together the butter and sugar until light and fluffy.
2. Mix the instant coffee with one tablespoon of hot water, then add to the butter and sugar mixture.
3. Sift together the flour and cornstarch and add to the coffee mixture. Beat until smooth.
4. Place spoonfuls of the mixture onto a greased baking tray. Put into the refrigerator for ten minutes.
5. Bake in a 375°F (190°C) for about 15 minutes. Cool.

To freeze: When the cookies are cool, put into a plastic bag or wrap in aluminum foil. Seal, label and freeze.

To serve: Allow to thaw for about one hour at room temperature.

Jam Fingers

3½ cups cake flour	2 eggs
1 cup (250 g) butter	milk
grated rind of one lemon	jam
½ cup caster sugar	sugar

1. Butter an 7 × 10-inch (18 × 25-cm) tin.
2. Mix the butter into the flour, lemon rind and sugar.
3. Beat the eggs and add to the butter and flour mixture.
4. If the dough is too dry, add a little milk.
5. Halve the dough and roll out each piece to fit the tin.
6. Place one piece on the buttered tin and spread it with jam. Put the other piece on top. Brush with milk and sprinkle with sugar.
7. Bake in a 375°F 190°C) oven for about 20 minutes or until golden brown. Cut into fingers, remove from tin and cool.

To freeze: Wrap in aluminum foil. Seal, label and freeze.

To serve: Remove wrapping and thaw at room temperature for 1½ hours.

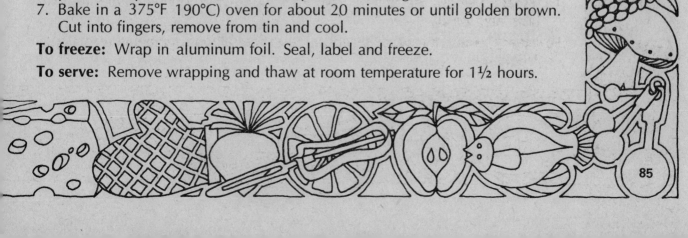

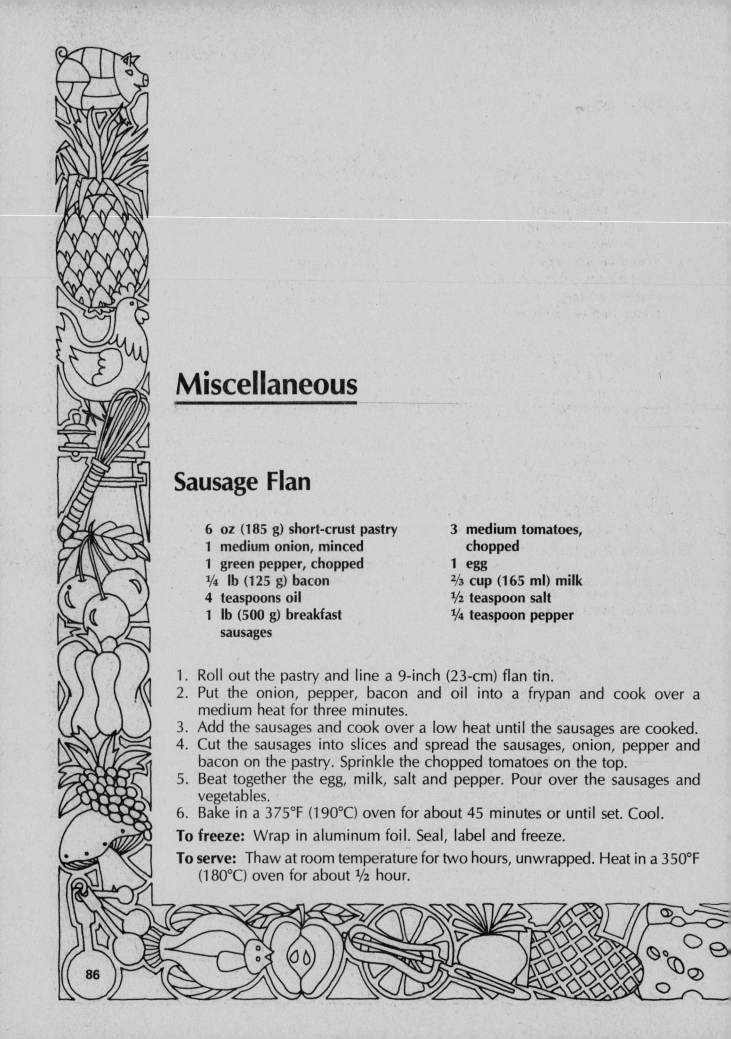

Miscellaneous

Sausage Flan

6 oz (185 g) short-crust pastry
1 medium onion, minced
1 green pepper, chopped
¼ lb (125 g) bacon
4 teaspoons oil
1 lb (500 g) breakfast
  sausages

3 medium tomatoes,
  chopped
1 egg
⅔ cup (165 ml) milk
½ teaspoon salt
¼ teaspoon pepper

1. Roll out the pastry and line a 9-inch (23-cm) flan tin.
2. Put the onion, pepper, bacon and oil into a frypan and cook over a medium heat for three minutes.
3. Add the sausages and cook over a low heat until the sausages are cooked.
4. Cut the sausages into slices and spread the sausages, onion, pepper and bacon on the pastry. Sprinkle the chopped tomatoes on the top.
5. Beat together the egg, milk, salt and pepper. Pour over the sausages and vegetables.
6. Bake in a 375°F (190°C) oven for about 45 minutes or until set. Cool.

To freeze: Wrap in aluminum foil. Seal, label and freeze.

To serve: Thaw at room temperature for two hours, unwrapped. Heat in a 350°F (180°C) oven for about ½ hour.

Mince Pies

Filling:
2 cooking apples, peeled, cored and grated
⅓ cup (60 g) raisins
⅓ cup (50 g) currants
2½ tablespoons mixed peel
⅓ cup brown sugar
1½ tablespoons melted butter
pinch of nutmeg
grated rind of one lemon

4 tablespoons lemon juice
egg white for glazing

Pastry:
2 cups (250 g) plain flour
1 teaspoon baking powder
¼ teaspoon salt
½ cup (125 g) butter
4-5 tablespoons ice water

1. Mix together all the filling ingredients. Set aside.
2. Make the pastry by sifting together the flour, baking powder and salt. Rub in the butter with your fingertips until the mixture looks like fine bread crumbs. Add the water, one tablespoon at a time, until a firm dough has formed.
3. Roll out the dough on a floured board and cut into rounds. Put half the rounds into buttered patty tins.
4. Fill with mincemeat and cover with the remaining rounds. Press edges together. Glaze with beaten egg white.
5. Bake in a 400°F (200°C) oven for about 15 minutes or until golden brown. Remove from tins and cool.

To freeze: Place in a plastic container in a single layer. Cover, seal, label and freeze.

To serve: Thaw at room temperature for about two hours. Heat in a 350°F (180°C) oven for ten minutes.

Boiled Rice

3 teaspoons salt
6 cups (1½ liters) boiling
   water
1 cup (210 g) short grain
   rice

1. Slowly pour the rice into the boiling salted water. Stir to ensure rice does not stick together.
2. Boil, uncovered, for 15 minutes.
3. Drain well and spread out to dry and cool.

To freeze: Put rice into a plastic container. Seal, label and freeze.

To serve: Put frozen rice (broken up) into boiling water. When the water returns to the boil, pour rice into a colander to drain and serve immediately.

Serves 4.

Fish Cakes

1 can (235 g) salmon
1 cup mashed potato
2 teaspoons lemon juice
2 tablespoons chopped
   parsley

salt and pepper
plain flour
1 egg, beaten
bread crumbs
oil for frying

1. Drain the salmon and mash in a bowl.
2. Add the potato, lemon juice and parsley. Season to taste with salt and pepper.
3. Form the mixture into small cakes.
4. Coat with flour, cover with egg and then toss in bread crumbs.
5. Heat the oil and fry the cakes until they are golden brown on both sides. Remove, drain and cool.

To freeze: Wrap the cakes in aluminum foil and put in a plastic container. Seal, label and freeze.

To serve: Reheat in a 350°F (180°C) oven for about ½ hour without thawing.

Pizza

1 cup plain flour	6 anchovy fillets
¼ teaspoon salt	¼ lb (125 g) Mozzarella
2 teaspoons dried yeast	cheese
⅓ cup (85 ml) warm water	1 teaspoon oregano
4 tomatoes, peeled and	½ cup chopped ham
chopped	salt and pepper
½ cup (125 g) tomato paste	2 teaspoons oil

1. Sift the flour into a warm bowl with the salt.
2. Put the yeast into a small bowl and add the warm water. Allow to stand for five minutes, then mix until smooth.
3. Pour the yeast mixture onto the flour and mix to a stiff dough. Knead on a floured board for five minutes. Put into an oiled bowl, cover with a cloth and leave in a warm place for about two hours or until the dough doubles in size. Roll out to a thickness of ¼ inch (5 mm).
4. Spread evenly with tomato paste.
5. Arrange the tomatoes, anchovy fillets and slices of cheese on the pizza dough. Sprinkle with oregano, chopped ham, salt and pepper to taste and oil.
6. Bake in a 425°F (220°C) oven for ½ hour. Cool.

To freeze: Wrap the cooled pizza in aluminum foil. Seal tightly, label and freeze.

To serve: Unwrap the pizza and thaw at room temperature for about one hour. Heat in a 375°F (190°C) oven for 20 minutes.

Serves 2.

Cornish Pasties

Filling:
1 lb (500 g) ground beef
2 small onions, chopped
2 medium potatoes, chopped
1 medium carrot, chopped
1 small turnip, chopped
1½ tablespoons chopped parsley
2 teaspoons salt

½ teaspoon pepper
¼ cup (65 ml) water

Pastry:
4 cups (500 g) plain flour
2 teaspoons baking powder
½ teaspoon salt
1 cup (250 g) butter
½ cup (125 ml) ice water
beaten egg yolk for glazing

1. Mix together all the ingredients for the filling. Set aside.
2. Make the pastry by sifting together the flour, baking powder and salt. Rub in the butter with your fingertips until the mixture is the consistency of bread crumbs. Gradually add the water until a firm dough is formed.
3. Divide the pastry into ten parts and roll out each portion. Place a saucer on the dough and trim around the edges.
4. Divide the filling into ten and put a portion on each pastry round.
5. Fold in half and pinch the edges together.
6. Place on a baking tray, prick with a knife to let the steam escape and glaze with the beaten egg yolk.
7. Bake in a 400°F (200°C) oven for ten minutes. Reduce the oven to 350°F (180°C) and bake for another ½ hour. Remove from the oven and cool.

To freeze: Put into individual plastic bags, seal, label and freeze.

To serve: Thaw in plastic bags overnight or for 12 hours.

Sausage Rolls

1 lb (500 g) sausage meat
1½ tablespoons chopped
   parsley
2 tablespoons plain flour
¼ teaspoon pepper
1½ teaspoons salt

½ teaspoon crushed bay
   leaves
¼ teaspoon rosemary
⅓ cup (85 ml) water
1 lb (500 g) puff pastry

1. Mix together the sausage mince, chopped parsley, flour, pepper, salt, crushed bay leaves, rosemary and water.
2. Put into a saucepan and cook over a medium heat, stirring constantly, for five minutes.
3. Roll out pastry to a thickness of ⅛ inch (3 mm) and cut in squares. Spoon meat mixture onto each square. Fold one edge of the pastry onto the meat then overlap with the other side. Pinch the edges together. (You may glaze the rolls with milk or egg.)
4. Bake in a 350°F (180°C) oven for about 20 minutes or until golden brown. Cool.

To freeze: Put one layer of sausage rolls on a tray and put in freezer uncovered for two hours. Then put in a plastic bag or plastic container. Seal, label and return to the freezer. You may also freeze uncooked sausage rolls in the same way.

To serve: Thaw cooked sausage rolls in their wrapping in the refrigerator for about 5 hours. Heat in a 400°F (200°C) oven for 20 minutes. If sausage rolls are uncooked, thaw at room temperature for about 15 minutes and bake in a 475°F (250°C) oven for about 20 minutes.

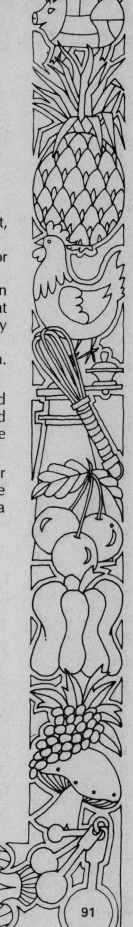

Cheese Straws

1 cup plain flour	¾ cup grated Parmesan
¼ teaspoon dry mustard	cheese
¼ teaspoon salt	1 egg yolk
pinch of cayenne	2 teaspoons water
5 tablespoons (75 g) butter	

1. Sift together the flour, mustard, salt and cayenne.
2. Mash the butter until very soft.
3. Add the dry ingredients to the butter with the cheese.
4. Beat the egg yolk with the water and add to the flour, butter and cheese mixture. Mix well to a firm dough. Add a little more water if necessary.
5. Roll out thinly on a floured board and cut into straws (approximately 5 mm by 10 cm).
6. Put on a greased baking tray and bake in a 350°F (180°C) oven for ten minutes. Remove from baking tray and cool on a wire rack.

To freeze: Wrap in a plastic cling wrap and put in an airtight plastic container or plastic bag. Seal well, label and freeze.

To serve: Leave the Cheese Straws in their wrappings and thaw at room temperature for at least one hour.

Doughnuts

2 cups plain flour	2 eggs, lightly beaten
2 teaspoons baking powder	oil for deep frying
4 tablespoons (60 g) butter	sugar
¼ cup sugar	

1. Sift the flour and baking powder into a large bowl.
2. Mix in the butter.
3. Add the sugar and mix well.
4. Add the eggs and beat well. (The dough should be stiff, but if it is too dry and not holding together, add a little milk.)
5. Roll out to a thickness of ½ inch (one cm) and cut into rounds.
6. Deep fry in the hot oil until they rise to the top and are golden brown. Drain on absorbent paper and coat with sugar. Cool.

To freeze: Wrap in aluminum foil in one layer. Seal, label and freeze.

To serve: Thaw at room temperature, unwrapped, for about two hours. Or heat in a 350°F (180°C) oven.

Croissants

4 teaspoons dried yeast	1 teaspoon salt
1 cup (250 ml) warm milk	3 tablespoons (45 g) melted
¾ cup (185 ml) warm water	butter
1 teaspoon sugar	1 cup (250 g) butter
4 cups plain flour	1 egg, beaten

1. Put the dried yeast, milk, water and sugar into a bowl. Mix once and leave for ten minutes.
2. Sift the flour and salt into a large bowl and add the yeast mixture and the melted butter. Mix well, then knead to a smooth dough. Refrigerate for ½ hours.
3. Divide the butter into three pieces and roll out the dough to a rectangle 7 × 22 inches (18 × 55 cm).
4. Spread one piece of the butter onto ⅔ of the dough. Fold the unbuttered ⅓ onto the buttered section. Fold the other ⅓ of the buttered section on top. You will end up with a three-layered envelope with butter between each layer. Refrigerate for 15 minutes.
5. Repeat step 4 two more times until the butter has all been used.
6. Divide the dough into four equal pieces. Roll each piece to a rectangle 9 × 18 inches (23 × 45 cm). Cut each rectangle into five triangles. Roll up from the base to the point and form into a crescent.
7. Place on a buttered baking tray and leave to rise in a warm place for ½ hour. Brush with the beaten egg and bake in a 450°F (230°C) oven for about 10 minutes. Cool.

To freeze: Wrap in aluminum foil or put into a plastic bag. Seal, label and freeze.

To serve: Place frozen croissants in a 350°F (180°C) oven until warm through.

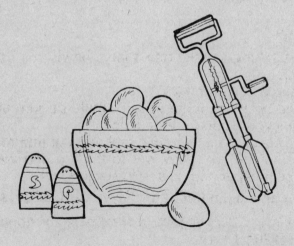

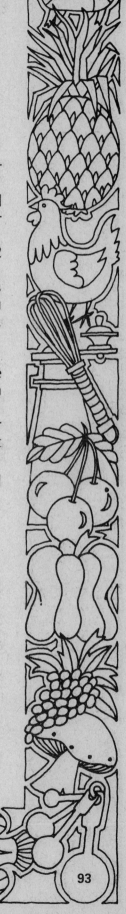

Biscuits

2 ¾ cups cake flour
pinch of salt
½ cup (125 g) butter
½ cup sugar
1 egg, slightly beaten
milk

1. Sift the flour and salt into a large bowl.
2. Mix in the butter until the mixture is the consistency of bread crumbs.
3. Add the sugar and the egg.
4. Mix in only enough milk to form a soft dough.
5. Knead the dough for a couple of minutes on a floured board.
6. Roll out to a thickness of ½ inch (one cm). Cut into rounds.
7. Put on a greased baking tray and cook in a 400°F (200°C) oven for about 12 minutes. Cool.

To freeze: Wrap in aluminum foil or put into a plastic bag. Seal, label and freeze.

To serve: Thaw at room temperature for about one hour or heat the frozen scones in a 350°F (180°C) oven.

Index

FR–B8096–3/69